Letts

Face Value

Drama Frames

Playscript and resources by
Adrian Lockwood and Kelvin Reynolds

Dedicated to Frances Bowen Day

Series editors

Matthew O'Neill and Jo O'Neill

Published by Letts Educational
The Chiswick Centre
414 Chiswick High Road
London W4 5TF
Tel: 020 89963333
Fax: 020 87428390
Email: mail@lettsed.co.uk
Website: www.letts-education.com

Letts Educational is part of the Granada Learning Group. Granada Learning is a division of Granada plc.

First published 2004

ISBN 1844190242

British Library Cataloguing in Publication Data
A catalogue record for this book is available from the British Library.

Acknowledgements
The publishers would like to thank the following for permission to use copyright material. Every effort has been made to trace copyright holders and to obtain their permission for the use of copyright material. The author and publishers will gladly receive information enabling them to rectify any error or omission in subsequent editions.
p79 Reproduced from *An Inspector Calls* by J.B. Priestley (copyright © Estate of J.B. Priestley 1947) is reproduced by kind permission of PFD on behalf of the estate of J.B. Priestley; p80 *Night & Day* magazine, The Daily Mail© Atlantic Syndication

Commissioned by Helen Clark
Project management by Julia Swales
Editing by Helen Clark, Matthew O'Neill and Jo O'Neill, Vicky Butt and Julia Swales
Cover design by Bigtop
Internal design by Bigtop
Internal layout by Hart McLeod, Cambridge
Production by PDQ
Printed and bound by Canale, Italy

Contents

Key to icons

 cross-reference from
play to resources

 cross-reference from
resources to play

 homework

Key to Framework objectives

S&L	Speaking and listening	W	Writing
		R	Reading

Characters

Students

All students are approximately fourteen to fifteen years old.

DJ (Destiny Jade)	An egotist, wants to be famous.
Russell	A dreamer who doesn't quite fit the mould.
Craig	A bully.
Ruby	A 'friend' of DJ's. Insecure, helpful, supportive, tries to please everyone.
Yasmin and Kia	DJ's friends.
Anthony	Russell's friend.
Dexter, Smithie and Roy	Craig's gang.
Extras	Students.

Teachers and workers in the school

Mrs King	The Principal, mid-forties.
Mr Max Lucas	Drama teacher, early forties.
Mrs Kathy Hayes	Form tutor, early thirties.

Miss Jane Parker	English teacher, late twenties.
Miss Lynda Hamilton	Biology teacher, thirties.
Mr David Collins	New English teacher, early thirties.
Mrs Renee Mortimer	Canteen assistant, fifties.

Characters in daydream sequences

Rod	DJ's manager.
Lola	DJ's PA.
Ben Shepherd	Television presenter.
Carl	DJ's bodyguard.
Phil	Cockney chef.

Russell II

Four models

Extras for crowd scenes

Acknowledgements

The authors would like to thank the following people for their help and advice: June Cannie, Principal at Sawston Village College, Sawston, Cambridge; Janet McNeill; Laura O'Keefe; Susan Elkin; Anna Johnson; Susan Reynolds; Shane Reynolds and members of the Creative Drama Group, Sawston Village College, Cambridge.

Scene 1: Brad Wolf

69
76

Stage semi-lit, 'danger' music (James Bond theme). A dark figure walks onto the stage and two other figures surround him threateningly. He quickly terminates them with a swift series of martial art moves. The figure comes front stage out of the shadow. He stands confidently.

RUSSELL *(in a deep, masculine voice)* Name's Wolf, Brad Wolf, deep cover espionage agent, protector of the innocent and lover of … beautiful women. It's a tough job but someone's got to do it. *(in normal voice)* Okay, okay, stop music! *('danger' music stops)* Not quite slick enough. Let's try again.

Cue 'danger' music again. 'Brad Wolf' walks on in the same manner. The two thugs charge towards him from either side of the stage. 'Brad' changes direction and without doing anything the two goons collide, knocking each other unconscious. 'Brad', front stage, dusts his hands off.

RUSSELL *(in deep, masculine voice)* Name's Wolf. Brad W… *(he is interrupted)*

ANTHONY Hey Russ, what're you doing?

RUSSELL *(looking sheepish and embarrassed)* Er, nothing. Nothing at all. Just, er, taking in the scenery.

ANTHONY Of your bedroom?! Looked like you were playing 'Super-fly-sexy-lover-of-women' again!

RUSSELL *(putting on an outraged look)* How dare you accuse me of such a puerile and despicable act.

ANTHONY Russ, when you start using big words like that, I know we're in trouble!

RUSSELL Okay! Okay! If you must know, I've done it again!

ANTHONY   What have you done? Started an international incident? Assassinated the wrong dictator?

RUSSELL   I'm in love!

ANTHONY   Uh oh. It's worse than I thought.

RUSSELL   Her name is DJ.

ANTHONY   You're in love with a DJ? Does she have her own decks?

RUSSELL   No, her name is DJ.

ANTHONY   You're in love with someone called 'DJ'?!

RUSSELL   Her actual name is … Destiny Jade. (*has a far away 'lost in love' look in his eyes*)

ANTHONY   (*flabbergasted*) Destiny Jade?! And which planet did you say she came from? Is this Destiny Jade of the Seventh Dimension, or is it Destiny Jade Vampire Slayer. (*bursts out laughing uncontrollably*)

RUSSELL   You have absolutely no appreciation of the finer feelings, my moronic friend.

ANTHONY   (*composing himself*) Okay. Seriously. You haven't exactly got a great track record. Now remember Lizzie Atkinson and that whole thing with the secret notes, pretending you were someone else. What a mess that was! Why didn't you just tell her you liked her and see if she liked you?

RUSSELL   It's not so simple, and anyway, that was different. This time it's real. I will claim my Destiny!

ANTHONY   (*rolling his eyes*) Oh boy!

Lights fade.

Scene 2: The big event

73
76

School corridor. Small group gathered around a notice-board. DJ is holding a mobile phone, chatting to Yasmin. Ruby is studiously writing notes from the board onto a pad. Russ and two friends are standing stage right chatting.

DJ Oh my GOD! It was like, sooooooo embarrassing! You should have seen what she was wearing! It was sooooooo Year 7, soooooooo last season. I mean, like, who wears ORANGE anymore?! And I'm standing there right next to her! (*looking shocked*)

YASMIN (*whispering urgently*) Shhhh! Look, she's right over there. (*points to **Ruby** who is studying the notice-board*) At least she's not wearing that orange top.

DJ Shame about the face though.

*They both burst into giggles. **Ruby** turns around. They go over to her with fake smiles on their faces.*

DJ Oh hi Ruby, I was just telling Yasmin about that *lovely* top you were wearing. (***DJ** and **Yasmin** exchange glances and **Yasmin** tries to stop herself giggling*) Anyway, what are you up to?

RUBY Oh nothing!

DJ What's this? (*takes **Ruby's** pad out of her hand and then reads aloud*) 'School play' … 'drama competition' … blah, blah, blah … Big deal, so what? (*hands pad back*)

RUBY Well, er, there's a prize for the best script.

DJ (*unenthusiastically*) Oh wow.

YASMIN (*looking at the notice-board, excitedly*) Wait a

8

minute. Look! There's a prize for Best Actress AND a free photo shoot AND …

DJ … it's going to be on TV. (*looking at Ruby*) Well, might be interested in your play after all.

RUBY (*looking put out and irritated*) But, er …

DJ Go on then, put our names down.

DJ and Yasmin turn and walk away. Ruby stays next to the notice-board.

RUBY But, er …

DJ Wonder if there's a prize for the best orange top?

DJ and Yasmin giggle and stand stage left gossiping. Russ steps away from his group of friends looking across the stage at DJ.

RUSS There she is! My Destiny! DJ, a vision from heaven, a goddess walking upon the earth. (*he falls to his knees*) Now is our chance to be together, our destinies can become one, we will be united forever. (*looks at Ruby*) Sign me up NOW! I will be her prince!

Ruby sighs and reluctantly writes his name down – lights go down.

Scene 3: The alpha female

DJ returns and is picked out by spotlight. She stands in front of 'image tree', a totem pole structure with various objects hanging from it, e.g. trainers, bags, earrings, tops, skirts, caps, logos. (An alternative could be an 'image altar table'.) She looks at Ruby and Russ, frozen, still standing next to the notice-board, with mixture of pity and contempt.

DJ   Pathetic, isn't it? But we do have one thing in common, we both worship me. (*pause*) Well, that's not quite true, there are other things I worship. The Great God Image. Bling Bling! It's like Christmas every day for me here. *(DJ surveys pole or 'altar table' with various objects on it)*

Oh my God, this top is sooo amazing, I just love this ... and those heels ... woow! And this bag, simply must have! *(DJ gets carried away – then notices **Ruby**)*

Don't feel sorry for her. I mean image is everything. It's all about the haves and the have nots – it's all about money isn't it? But if you can't afford the latest pair of trainers, here's a little tip, put them through the washing machine, no-one will notice the difference – for a while. *(picks up trainers, then picks up small top and throws towards **Ruby**)*

Here Ruby, try this, it's last year's brown but it will do for you. *(leaves image table and walks to front of stage)*

It's not just about what you wear. You gotta walk the walk and talk the talk if you wanna be King Girl. Confidence is everything. Don't look down, don't look away, look straight ahead. Oh and charisma, you gotta have charisma, and charm. Know who you're talking to, that's important. 'Hi Mr Producer, you noticing me!' *(pouts and poses)* It's a gift, use it wisely. Smile sweetly when you have to, flutter your eyelids, play the vulnerable. Works every time. But take no prisoners. It's dog eat dog in this world. Strike when you have to, be ruthless. One day I shall be up there, a rich and famous celeb., that's my destiny, my game plan. Image is everything, looks are everything and above all it's confidence, confidence, confidence. And if you haven't got that you better pray for a nice personality. (*looks at Ruby again*) You know I'm right. I didn't make the rules, I just play the game to win. (*DJ tosses hair, leaves stage, then stops and turns*) Oh and remember what the philosopher said, 'Before you can love others, you must first learn to love yourself.'

Scene 4: Be a man

School playground before the bell goes. There are various groups of pupils milling around, including Craig and some other boys. Russ is on his way to his form room with Anthony.

CRAIG   (*talking to his group of friends*) Yeah, so I kicked his head in didn't I, just like on that film we saw.

DEXTER   'Cos he didn't give you no respec'?

SMITHIE   You the MAN!

DEXTER   Yeah, you the MAN!

Russell and Anthony walk by.

RUSSELL   So there she was, like a vision, like a …

ANTHONY   OK, enough already! So that's the reason you're going to be in this play, so you can be with her? So you can make a complete fool out of yourself?

RUSSELL   She is the princess of pulchritude, my perfect paramour! Her divine beauty will inspire me to be the greatest actor!

ANTHONY   Uh oh. There go those big words again. Now I know we're in trouble … or should I say, YOU'RE in trouble. I'm having nothing to do with this.

RUSSELL Ant, you just wouldn't understand.

ANTHONY What I don't understand is who you're trying to be now. Let's face it, whether you're going to be an actor or not, you're always acting. Anyway, I'll see you later. I've got to give in my Maths homework.

Anthony is just about to leave when Craig and his mates block their way.

CRAIG You *girls* alright?

ANTHONY Yeah, fine. We're busy, so, er, see ya. (*Anthony tries to move but Craig blocks his way*)

CRAIG I hear you girls are in a play. 'Bit girlie don't you think? I mean, call yourself a bloke?

RUSSELL Listen you … you moron, if you don't move I will be forced to teach you a lesson.

CRAIG (*threateningly*) What lesson?

RUSSELL (*in movie hero type voice*) One you won't forget.

He makes a few fancy kung-fu type moves, which are over the top and unconvincing. Dexter and Smithie burst out laughing. Anthony has his head in his hands.

ANTHONY (*exasperated*) Oh boy! OK, time out! Russell, we really have to be going. (*grabs Russell's arm and tries to drag him away but again he is blocked by Craig*)

CRAIG What's the matter? Not man enough to fight?

RUSSELL I'll fight ya! Let me at 'im Ant! (*Anthony holds him back*)

CRAIG Come on, be a man.

RUSSELL I'm trying to be but he won't let me. (*tries to get in front of **Anthony** who continues to hold him back*)

ANTHONY OK, what is it that you want, Crags?

CRAIG Your attention. Your respect.

ANTHONY You've got it. Respect-respect-respect … all for you. There. Now we're going. (*grabs **Russell** and quickly pushes past **Craig***)

CRAIG That's right, you girls go run back to your little girlie plays. (*in a squeaky voice*) 'Ooh, look at me. I can act.' (***Dexter** and **Smithie** fall about laughing*)

RUSSELL Why didn't you fight him? He's a bully.

ANTHONY Because I want to survive.

RUSSELL I would have taken him, no problem. I saw how to do it on this film …

ANTHONY You *really* need a reality check, Russ. This isn't a film. He would have pounded you into mincemeat.

RUSSELL But it was embarrassing backing down like that. What's that gonna do for my image?

ANTHONY Russ, I don't mean to point out the obvious, but if you want to be a hero you don't always get out in one piece; people get hurt, things get broken, the ending isn't always the one you were looking for. Hanging around with you is getting far too weird, I'm going.

*Exit **Anthony** – lights fade.*

Scene 5: Insignificant mortal

*Lights up. **Russell** is in his room next to a full-length standing mirror. He has a men's health magazine in his hands with a title like 'Pumping Iron' or 'Made for Men'. He begins posing in front of the mirror, flexing his muscles and comparing himself to the magazine pictures. He makes one final dramatic pose, straining all his muscles excessively, when he suddenly gets cramp and staggers to a chair exhausted with the effort. When he recovers he flicks through the magazine.*

RUSSELL Bulging muscles. Rugged good looks. Charming, stylish and cool. (*he looks at his own feeble muscles and looks exasperated*) People notice someone like that. That kind of person stands out in the crowd. That kind of person gets what he wants. Uh oh! I feel a daydream coming on …

*Two athletic male figures walk onstage in an exaggerated, 'macho' manner. They stand at each side of **Russell**. He looks at them and sighs forlornly.*

RUSSELL If I could look like them my problems would be over. I'd be invited to every party, be chosen for every team and … I'd be popular. Everyone would like me.

*Two girls walk by and **Russell**, very interested, stands up.*

RUSSELL Hey, WOW! This daydream just got a lot better! (*to the girls*) Hi ladies, I'm Russell, but you can call me Russ … (*the girls push him back down on the chair, then drape themselves admiringly around the athletic-looking males*)

RUSSELL See what I mean? (*talking to the athletic males* *and the girls*) Okay you guys, daydream's over, get out of my room!

They turn and go off stage. **Russell** *faces the audience.*

RUSSELL The problem, if you want to know, is ME. Yup, me. Good ol' Russell Winter. The name just about says it all: 'He's simple', 'He's ordinary', 'He's BORING!' It's not good enough. Maybe I'm not good enough. I want to be noticed. I want to be the tall, dark, handsome, and mysterious guy that everyone wants to be seen with. So, from now on things are going to change! I'm going for the complete Russ make-over, a Russ re-fit, a brand new Russ of unbelievable cool and sophistication who will bring the school to its knees. (*laughs a frenzied, demented, horror movie laugh*) Then, Destiny Jade will be mine … (*he pauses and reconsiders*) … well, she might just speak to me … maybe …

Lights fade.

Scene 6: Russ re-fitted

Russell's form room in the morning, before the form tutor has arrived. There are several pupils there, some sitting and others standing about chatting. Enter **Russell**. *He has his collar up and top two shirt buttons undone. He is wearing sunglasses and swaggers into the room hoping that everyone sees him. Unfortunately, because of the sunglasses, he walks painfully into a table. He hurriedly removes the glasses and composes himself, then sidles up to a group of girls and begins combing his hair in long, dramatic strokes. The girls look at each other in disbelief.*

GIRL 1 What are you doing, Russell?

RUSSELL That's Russ to you, baby-cakes.

The girls snigger.

GIRL 1 Don't 'baby-cakes' me you twerp.

RUSSELL Hey, take a chill-pill girl! Just cool your jets and let ol' daddy here know what's going down, what's the buzz, what's the scene … baby … cakes!

GIRL 2 What language are you speaking Russ?!

GIRL 3 Yeah. Go back to your own planet, weirdo.

RUSSELL That's cool, 'cos Russ the Man knows when the ladies are overwhelmed by his powerful presence. I'll see YOU (*pointing at the girls*) … later.

*The morning bell goes. **Russell** turns to go to his desk and falls dramatically over a chair he hadn't realised was behind him. He quickly retrieves himself and staggers to his desk. **Mrs Hayes**, the form tutor, enters. **Russell** coolly puts on his shades again and places his feet lazily on the chair next to him.*

MRS HAYES Right you lot, settle down now. Let's do the register. Helen?

GIRL 1 Yes miss.

MRS HAYES Tanya?

GIRL 2 Yes miss.

MRS HAYES Russell?

RUSSELL That's my name. Just don't wear it out, 'cos I gotta use it.

***Mrs Hayes** looks up and really sees **Russell** for the first time.*

MRS HAYES Russell, get your feet off the chair. Why are you wearing sunglasses in my classroom?

RUSSELL Well, my future's so bright I gotta wear shades. (*big smile on his face – the rest of the class are either in disbelief or embarrassed for him*)

MRS HAYES Your future, young man, is looking *very* uncertain from where I'm standing. (*shouting*) NOW GET OUT OF MY CLASS!

Russell looks petrified. He turns to the audience.

RUSSELL Okay, FREEZE! FREEZE!

The class scene behind freezes. Russell steps out of the scene.

Now that WASN'T supposed to happen. According to my calculations the outcome was meant to be different. 'Cool' is meant to dazzle everyone, 'cool' is meant to make them *like* you, 'cool' always wins. Now, this is the way it *should* have been. Okay, REWIND!

The classroom scene behind goes back to exactly the way it was at the start of the scene. Russell walks in looking 'cool'. All the girls swoon in an over-exaggerated manner and gather around him and the boys look on admiringly.

GIRL 1 How are you doing, Russ? You remember me don't you?

GIRL 2 Hey, I saw him first.

RUSSELL Ladies, one at a time, please.

GIRL 3 Ooooh, I just love how he takes control.

*Enter the form tutor, **Mrs Hayes**. She comes up to **Russell** rather shyly.*

MRS HAYES (*rather nervously*) Er, Russ? I've, er, been thinking about what you said the other day. You know, about getting rid of homework? Well, I think it's an excellent idea and we're going to implement some of the policies you drafted the other day. I hope you find this agreeable, but if there are any problems then just come and see us and we'll put it right immediately.

GIRLS No more homework?! Russ, you're just so COOL!

RUSSELL Well done Mrs Hayes. I think it's time you took the register, don't you?

MRS HAYES Oh yes, yes of course. And I'd just like to say Russ, it's a privilege for me to have you in my form.

The scene freezes. ***Russell*** *steps out and addresses the audience.*

RUSSELL Now that's how it should have worked. Instead, I've been humiliated and I'm in detention. I don't understand. What went wrong? I've got to figure this image thing out. Maybe it's time for some adjustments to the 'cool' formula.

Scene 7: Cheeky

A school corridor between lessons. ***Craig*** *has a mobile phone in his hand and is checking a text message.* ***Smithie***, ***Dexter*** *and a few other boys are gathered around him. They are in no hurry to get to the next lesson.*

SMITHIE Got any fags on ya, Crags?

CRAIG What's it to ya?

SMITHIE Well give us some then.

CRAIG It'll cost ya.

DEXTER Look out, staff comin'.

Mr Collins, a new teacher, approaches.

MR COLLINS Come on you lot, the bell went ages ago. Let's get to classes.

The boys make to move, except Craig who remains looking at his text message. Mr Collins approaches.

MR COLLINS Come on, you're late.

SMITHIE Yeah, yeah, we're going. (*they go reluctantly but Craig stays put – the others double back to see what is going to happen*)

MR COLLINS (*to Craig*) Well, are you going or …

CRAIG (*looking at his mobile phone and not the teacher*) I'm busy. Just checkin' my messages ain't I?

MR COLLINS Get to your lesson NOW.

CRAIG (*still refusing to look up*) Yeah, yeah, keep yer hair on.

The other boys are laughing behind Mr Collins. Craig is aware of his audience and shoots them a sly smile.

MR COLLINS Look at me when I'm talking to you.

CRAIG Why should I? You interrupted me in the middle of something important. I thought you was one of them poncey Year 7s, didn't I.

The other boys laugh. Craig has a smile on his face, and is now staring Mr Collins right in the eyes.

MR COLLINS Right, that's enough. What's your name?

CRAIG What's yours?

MR COLLINS That's it …

CRAIG 'Cos you've gotta be careful who you speak to these days … don't ya.

*The principal, **Mrs King** walks in. The other boys rapidly leave the scene. **Craig** suddenly realises he's lost his audience and his composure changes, he seems almost to shrink.*

CRAIG (*less confident*) OK, I … er, don't want to be late for my lesson. (*he starts to go but **Mr Collins** blocks his path*)

MR COLLINS Not so fast …

MRS KING Is there a problem, Mr Collins?

MR COLLINS This young man decided to give me a lot of back-chat and refused to tell me his name.

MRS KING Is that true, Craig?

CRAIG (*nervous now*) I … er, it was a mistake. I was just going when …

MRS KING And is that a mobile phone in your hand? You know they're banned in school, don't you? Come on, let's have it. (*puts her hand out for it*)

CRAIG (*refusing to hand it over*) I can't. It's, er, not mine …

MRS KING Right, let's have you in my office. Right now.

Lights fade.

Scene 8: Be hard

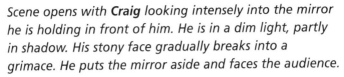

*Scene opens with **Craig** looking intensely into the mirror he is holding in front of him. He is in a dim light, partly in shadow. His stony face gradually breaks into a grimace. He puts the mirror aside and faces the audience.*

CRAIG   Hard. Hard as rock. Hard as granite. Hard as steel. I am. Always will be. No one comes close, no one comes near. Don't want 'em near. Keep your distance. Back off. Leave me alone. Come any closer an' I'll 'ave ya. Good innit? Effective. To the point. I've practised it to perfection. (*turns the mirror to face himself and talks to it, aggressively*) Whatta you lookin' at? Come on then, bring it on, bring it on … (*turns mirror to face the audience*) Now take a look at the lot of ya. Soft, that's what you are, soft. Pathetic. And what do you think you're looking at? Don't look at me sunshine. My eyes will burn holes through you, burn holes through glass … (*flips the mirror around and stares into it momentarily, then faces the audience with a grin*) It's my shell. The one I've made. It's my armour. Nobody gets through, nobody gets near.

Lights fade.

Scene 9: Lessons

*Year 10 English class. Group work. **Anthony, Roy, Russ, Yasmin, DJ** and **Ruby** are seated at one table, looking at various cards in front of them on the desk.*

ANT   Come on then, we better get on with it, don't want to be sitting here at lunchtime.

ROY   All right, so what we got so far then?

ANT First … (*shuffling cards*) we have to create the perfect female.

ROY That should be easy … just write down that blonde tennis player everyone is talking about.

ANT Yeah! Or …

YASMIN (*snatches up paper and reads*) 'Girls that are fit'. This is pathetic.

DJ OK then, so … we'll have guys that are fit.

YASMIN Good idea! Right who should we put down?

RUBY Look, this isn't what we're supposed to be doing, making up stupid lists about who's fit and who isn't. I don't want to stay in at lunchtime even if you do.

DJ All right, all right! Don't get stressed. They started it, going on about that stupid tennis player.

ANT Shut up, you're just jealous, cos you don't look like her.

DJ Excuse me? I do not want to be another glamourous tennis star. I want to be the first Destiny Jade! (*sounds of oohhh from others*) OK, you can laugh now, but you'll see. (*getting up*)

RUBY Where are you going?

DJ (*in a low voice*) To talk to Russ. He's going to help me with my history essay, but he doesn't know it yet.

RUBY (*sighs*) Suppose I'll have to sort this out then!

DJ (*slides in empty seat beside **Russ**, who shifts uncomfortably*) Hi babes, how you doing?

RUSSELL (*nervous*) I'm … eh … (*mutters to himself*) OK,

OK be cool. (*out loud*) All right. (*carries on writing, pretends to be unconcerned*) What do you want?

DJ Well you know that essay on factory life that has to be in today.

RUSSELL Umm … sort of.

DJ Can you believe it? I've gone and left all my notes at home and if I don't get it in today Jones will kill me. Don't suppose I could borrow yours and copy it up at lunchtime, I mean I won't copy it word for word, just the basics.

RUSSELL (*looks up … pulls essay from his folder, hesitates*) I dunno.

DJ Oh pleeeaaase, Russ, you don't want to get me into trouble do you? Look you can have my chocky bar if you like, that's fair. (*gives him bar of chocolate*) and … I hear you want to take me to the Leavers' Ball next year.

RUSSELL What!! Who told you that?

DJ Someone said … but of course if you don't want to …

RUSSELL No … Yeah, that's cool! Here, I wouldn't want to let a girl down. (**DJ** *smiles and tucks essay in between her papers*)

DJ You're a star. (*breaks chocolate bar in half, puts some in her mouth, seductively*) Here, you have a piece. (**Russ** *goes all wobbly and is just about to take some when* **Miss Parker** *walks up to the desk*)

MISS PARKER Thank you very much. That's for me is it? (*snatches chocolate from* **DJ**) You know the rules, no eating in class.

DJ Ohh … Miss, I'm sorry, it's Russ's chocolate, he was

telling me all about it, apparently chocolate's really good for you, helps you concentrate, it's full of endorphins or something, puts you in a happy mood, doesn't it, Russ? We should all be eating loads of chocolate.

MISS PARKER   Well I don't care what it does, I'm having it now, and I'd be grateful if you'd go back to your group Destiny, as we've only got ten minutes left.

DJ resumes place with the others.

RUBY   What was that all about?

DJ   Tell you later.

MISS PARKER   Quiet! Now listen. I'm coming round giving every group an envelope. Inside there's a photograph. I would like you to make up a play or a story about being perfect. It must involve the person in your photo. (*starts handing out envelopes*)

ANT   Give us a good one, miss.

MISS PARKER   Um ... let's see, you've got sport, footballer.

ROY   Wicked!

RUBY   (*tuts*) Oh no.

YASMIN   It's OK, it's probably someone fit. (*opens envelope and removes photograph*) Who's this old fogey? (*disappointed*)

DJ   He looks about sixty.

ROY   Don't recognise him.

ANT   Miss Parker, who's this supposed to be?

MISS PARKER   That, Anthony, is George Best. One of the greatest footballers in the world, he used to play for

Manchester United.

ROY   Oh yeah, George Best, I've heard of him.

MISS PARKER   And in the sixties, he was more famous than any of the great young players of today.

DJ   Yeah but I'd still rather have Becks.

YASMIN   Yeah!

MISS PARKER   (*takes photo away*) All right then, you can have this one instead. (*hands **Ant** a second envelope*) I think you'll like this one.

ROY   Who have we got?

MISS PARKER   Two American film stars, beautiful females, young and very fit!

ROY   Oh nice one!

YASMIN   Oh no! ... We should have kept that football bloke.

ANT   (*opens new envelope*) Eh? What's this? Miss! This is wrong, we got dogs!

MISS PARKER   No you haven't got dogs, Anthony, they're wolves.

ROY   But ... (*confused*) you said we'd get American film stars.

ANT   Yeah, you said they were fit.

MISS PARKER   Well boys, say hello to Duma and Dakota, two American timber wolves. You can't get much fitter than that! Oh and they've been in loads of films and on TV. Just what you wanted, you said. And aren't they just the most beautiful creatures?

ROY Suppose.

YASMIN See, stupid! Now we've got landed with this. You and your big mouth. (*to Ant*)

MISS PARKER So to remind everyone, you have one week to write a story about perfection based on your group's photograph. OK. You can pack away now.

RUBY (*to others*) We can do something with this.

DJ (*packing away, to Yasmin*) Well I'm sorry, I'm not doing it. Why bother with perfection when you're looking at it! Are you coming to the canteen?

YASMIN (*laughs*) Yeah. God you're so vain, DJ!

DJ No I'm not, I'm just being realistic. Are you coming Ruby?

RUBY Well just for a bit. I had a sandwich at breaktime, and I've got some IT work to finish.

DJ Oh be a darling and make a copy of Russ's notes for me. Just type some of the main bits so it looks like my work, then I can hand it in after lunch. I would do it myself but I've got that dance rehearsal and you know how important that is.

RUBY But I've got loads to do and …

DJ (*hands over folder*) Ohhh … you're such a star, I'd give you my chocolate but Parker's just taken it. Tell you what, why don't you and Yasmin come round tonight and we can make a start on the story?

YASMIN Yeah, why not? We can have a good old girly gossip.

DJ and Yasmin saunter off.

RUBY (*sighs*) Thanks guys.

Scene 10: The canteen

Ruby follows DJ and Yasmin in a line by the counter looking at the various options of food and drink in front of her. Mrs Mortimer, the canteen assistant, is behind the counter serving the food. Craig is approaching from the back of the stage.

YASMIN Don't know what to have today, that apple crumble looks yummy.

DJ What's this? (*picking up can and putting it down again*) Benson's Cola? Haven't you got any Coke or Pepsi? (*to Mrs Mortimer*)

MRS MORTIMER No, sorry dear, that's all we've got. It's all the same anyway.

DJ No it's not, that's disgusting, I'm not drinking that.

MRS MORTIMER Go without then. (*DJ tuts and walks on, helping herself to a sandwich*)

RUBY (*looking at the sandwiches, mumbling to herself*) Chocolate spread, no, prawn mayonnaise, no, ... bacon and lettuce ... I don't know.

Suddenly Craig pushes her aside.

CRAIG (*to Ruby*) Come on out of the way big bum. (*shouts to friend*) 'Ere, get us a chicken burger.

MRS MORTIMER (*to Craig*) Do you mind not pushing in.

Craig grabs burger, smirks at Ruby and bites into burger then moves off and sits at another table with a few boys.

MRS MORTIMER Oh some people have got no manners. (*to Ruby*) Now then love, what can I get you?

RUBY It's OK, I'll just have ... umm ... these biscuits.

Ruby pays for lunch and joins DJ and Yasmin already seated at table eating lunch.

DJ   And she goes 'Oh Benson's Cola, it's just the same as the rest'. Yeah right, like she's some expert. (*leans over and pushes a spoon in Yasmin's crumble and tastes it*)

YASMIN   Oi! It's mine.

DJ   I've only had a spoonful, keep your hair on. (*to Ruby*) And what have you got? (*picks up her biscuits and reads side of packet*) 'Biscos – the ultra light snack for the girl on the go'. Ooooo Ruby, girl on the go, hey you're such a healthy eater! Are you on a diet or something?

RUBY   No. (*defensive*) I'm just not very hungry.

DJ   Wish I'd kept that chocolate now instead of giving it to Dimbo Russ.

YASMIN   But at least he did your history essay for you.

DJ   That's true. Good bit of business that.

RUBY   You're so lucky DJ, he wouldn't have done that for me.

DJ   You make your own luck in this world, sweetie, but you're right about one thing.

RUBY   What? (*DJ gets up and pushes her plate to one side, picks up bag*)

DJ   He wouldn't have done it for you. (*DJ smiles and leaves, aware of the looks she's getting from some of the boys*) Come on, dance class. Oh and Ruby, don't forget my essay, there's a sweetie. See ya.

YASMIN   Wait for me.

*Yasmin follows. **Ruby** sighs, eats a small portion of her biscuit and then puts it on the plate. She then collects up the other plates and makes a neat pile on the table, staring at them for a few seconds.*

Scene 11: The staffroom

*Lunchtime. Staff – **Max Lucas**, **Lynda Hamilton** and **Jane Parker** – relaxing in armchairs eating lunch.*

MAX   So what have you got in your tucker bag today then Lynda?

LYNDA   (*eating from container*) Homemade salad: leeks, greens, mushrooms, red cabbage, ummm … delicious, you should try some Jane.

JANE   No thanks! I would have to grow two long ears and call myself Bugsy if I was going to eat any of that stuff.

LYNDA   Actually it's very good for you.

JANE   So is chocolate, according to Destiny Jade Barnet.

MAX   What, 'Miss I love myself'?

JANE   Apparently. I just confiscated this from my Year 10 class and Destiny said (*imitates*) 'It's good for you miss, helps you concentrate, you can eat as much as you like'.

MAX   Destiny! What a bloody stupid name.

LYNDA   It's all right for her with her figure, sitting there smug, lecturing the rest of us. You wait till she's got three kids and stretch marks, she won't be so keen then to stuff her face with chocolate.

JANE   Oh dear. The bikini diet's not going too well, then?

LYNDA It's going very well. This salad is two points, then it's steamed fish and pasta for dinner tonight. Let's see … that's three points … that means I'll be in credit tomorrow.

JANE Hmmm. Eat, drink and be happy that's what I say.

LYNDA Yeah and that's probably why you're heading for a coronary.

MAX Well I look after myself. I was in the gym for an hour last night working out. We have that staff football match next week. I'm quite worried about it because I really don't feel in shape.

LYNDA But you went straight down the pub after the gym, so it was all a waste of time.

MAX But I only had a couple of mineral waters all evening. I am really watching what I eat too. I have been on a stupid diet for weeks.

JANE (*gets up and goes over to make some coffee*) You two have got to lighten up, you take things far too seriously. I mean Lynda, does it really matter if you wear a bikini or not in Malaga? You're on holiday, for goodness sake, you're supposed to be enjoying yourself not getting stressed out about what you look like. And Max, it is only a staff football match. I know that a lot of the blokes in the team are super-fit exercise freaks, but who cares what they think of you? You should both stop trying to be perfect.

LYNDA I'm not trying to be perfect, I'm just trying to be me. (*shows magazine*) Have you seen this, Max? Now she IS perfect. That dress is absolutely amazing. Have you seen the bloke on her arm too? He is gorgeous.

MAX Oh my God … and he's the same age as me.

JANE (*shouting across*) Who are we talking about here?

LYNDA Put it away, it's so depressing.

JANE It's just a photograph, Lynda. It's an image. You don't see her on a bad day. She's just an ordinary person underneath all that make up.

LYNDA Excuse me! She is not ordinary. My cousin stood next to her once in a bar in Edinburgh, and she said she's absolutely stunning. She looks even better in real life than she does in the photographs.

MAX She must be perfect then.

JANE There's no such thing. I mean the Greeks knew all about this quest for perfection. These Greek philosophers like Socrates used to go round the streets asking people questions about life, like what is beauty? What is truth? What is perfection?

MAX Sort of like an ancient market research.

JANE Sort of, yeah.

LYNDA And what answers did they come up with?

JANE Oh they didn't come up with any answers, they just asked the questions. Gave everyone something to think about. You see, there are always more questions than answers. The journey itself is more important than the destination.

LYNDA And the point of this riveting philosophical conversation is?

JANE (*returns to seat and picks up magazine*) Just saying, everyone's obsessed with this image thing. The celebrities in this magazine have got a whole army of people running around after them all day. Hairdressers, beauty therapists, style gurus, or whatever they're called, and I bet you anything there are days when they look in the mirror and think 'I look a right mess!'

LYNDA I think not.

MAX The media love this celeb thing, don't they? Look, there's one on every page! They can't go anywhere without someone pointing a camera at them. It's not real – it's like living your life in a bubble.

LYNDA I feel quite sorry for them really you know, these A-league celebs.

JANE Yeah, but the thing is they're not there for ever. They may be flavour of the month now but once their looks start to fade and the parts dry up, that's it. The public gets tired of them and the newspapers find someone else more interesting to write about. (*throws magazine down on table*)

LYNDA Like DJ, she wants to be an actress or a model or a pop star.

MAX Oh she'd love that wouldn't she? All that fame, all that attention. I can just see her now – Destiny Jade, the Hollywood teen princess.

LYNDA Dream on.

Scene 12: Hollywood dreams

70 *DJ sits at her bedroom dressing table applying make-up.*

76 **DJ** That's perfect. I'll show them at the disco! I'll show
78 them who's boss. (*she strikes a flamboyant pose in front*

of the mirror, then sits back staring into it) You have
got it. You can be … a star.

*DJ starts daydreaming. Lights come on illuminating the
whole stage. Music starts. DJ is now the superstar in her
dressing room. Enter her Personal Assistants, Rod and
Lola. DJ angrily brandishes a newspaper.*

DJ   Have you read this?

LOLA   (*a bit uncertain about what's going on*) Kind of …
I mean, it's not the showbiz page, it's not important.

DJ   Not important!? Not important!? Look what she said
about me! Look at it! (*thrusts newspaper in front of
Lola*) Read it, there, look! (*DJ quotes*) 'There's more to
see these days of model turned pop star Destiny Jade,
judging by the latest photo. The skin tight jeans do her
no favours but DJ, nineteen years old last month, could
soon be adding the title of 'Rear of the Year' to her
many other awards …' Who does she think she is?

ROD   Who wrote it?

LOLA   (*intimidated by DJ*) R … R … Rosie Batholomew.

DJ   The cow! Look at it! Covers most of page seven,
millions will see it, and you say it's not important!

ROD   We'll go for damage limitation.

DJ   You're supposed to stop this happening, that's what
you get paid for!

LOLA   Don't worry, we'll get a really good story in
tomorrow.

DJ   It's the last time she gets an interview from me,
jealous cow … I'll sue them.

LOLA   Yes, yes, of course. Whatever you say.

DJ It's like I've made it and she's having a go at me and she can't handle it because I've got the fame and the looks and she hasn't.

ROD That's right, honey.

DJ How could she say that about me? (*posing in mirror*) You don't really think I look that big do you?

LOLA No of course not, it's just a bad camera angle, that's all.

ROD You look great princess, trust me, there's no one better.

DJ Ahhh ... you're so sweet.

ROD Anyway, hasn't done JLo any harm, or Kylie. Look at all the good publicity they get.

LOLA Exactly. So do you want to look at the schedule for today?

DJ (*sighs and sits down*) Yeah, suppose so.

LOLA (*reads from clipboard*) Well after the TV interview, we go to the arena for rehearsal, then back here at five. I've ordered a light supper and ...

DJ Yeah and make sure I get the Marmite-flavoured crisps this time. I asked reception for them especially, and the stupid girl sent up cheese and onion. I mean, it's not exactly rocket science.

LOLA OK, we'll get that sorted. And then we're looking at lighting for the video shoot tomorrow. Oh, and we've got to squeeze in a 'meet the fans' slot downstairs in the lobby.

DJ Excuse me? I said I'd do the TV interview, but I never said I would do meet and greet! Hello!!?

LOLA   Well it's Rod's idea.

ROD   The manager said some of the fans have been waiting outside all night.

DJ   This is my time now, the fans don't own me, right? I'm not a piece of meat to be dragged around for everyone. They'll have to buy tickets to see the show like everyone else.

ROD   Yeah sure princess, I understand, but the cameras will be rolling for the interview, they can get a few shots of you and the fans beforehand, good for PR, especially after this. (*picks up newspaper*) Besides, it will only be for five minutes.

DJ   (*sighs heavily*) Right five minutes only and I want Karl beside me all the time.

LOLA   You got it.

DJ   OK, so who's doing the interview? Better not be that minger Rosie Bartholomew.

LOLA   It's Ben Shepherd.

DJ   Oh he's cute, I like him. So what it's gonna be? The strappy sandals or the red leather boots, what do you think?

LOLA   Well I like them both...

DJ   And tell the director I want soft focus lighting, it makes my hair look better.

*Hotel lobby. **DJ**, in dark glasses, plus **PR**s and bodyguard **Karl** move amongst the jostling crowd, and make token gestures to them. Cameras flash. **Karl** pushes fans out of* *the way. **DJ** poses for a couple of photos, photographers shouting out 'This way **DJ** … over here.' She moves through quickly to interview room where she sits down and has the stylist fussing round her, doing her make up. **Ben** enters, greets **DJ** and sits down.*

BEN Hi, lovely to see you, how are you?

DJ I'm fine.

BEN You look great, so er … in your time when you're ready.

ROD And don't forget, get a plug in for that charity lunch we're doing tomorrow.

BEN Let's roll. (*the show starts*) DJ, thank you so much for taking time out from your busy schedule to come and talk to us. We've managed to grab just a few moments.

DJ (*gushing smile*) No problem, I'm sorry I was late, I just had to stop and talk to all those fans out there … You know, some of them have been waiting all night.

BEN I know, we could hear them, the fans are obviously very important to you.

DJ Ben, they are my people, it's the least I can do.

BEN So Destiny Jade, pop star, model and actress, you've been described in one magazine as the most beautiful girl in the world. What's it like to wake up every morning with that title? Is it a burden you have to live with?

DJ (*fake, soft, American pie accent*) Oh my gosh! I never think of it like that. I'm just an ordinary girl who happens to be in films and videos, I don't go round all day saying 'Hey look at me, I'm so beautiful', these are just labels the media give you.

BEN   So do you spend ages in front of the mirror everyday? And you do look fabulous, I have to say.

DJ   Oh thank you, you're so sweet. No, I'm just like any other girl: I do my make up, I like my hair to look nice, that's it. It's not like I spend every minute of the day looking at myself in the mirror, obsessed if a hair's out of place or my dress is too tight … that's freaky. That's not me. (*giggles*)

BEN   Do you think being famous has changed you as a person?

DJ   Well, obviously I can't go shopping in the supermarkets anymore, and for security reasons, I have to be chauffeur-driven everywhere I go, but inside, have I changed? No. I'm still the same old DJ from the block because, Ben, the fans would see through me if I was artificial in any way. I'm just a basic, ordinary girl at heart who loves her family and her friends. This is my job. I happen to be a pop star and a model – it's what I do for a living – but hey, if it all changed tomorrow, I could be working in a shoe shop or a hairdressers and be just as happy because, Ben, it's what's inside that counts.

BEN   Destiny Jade, thank you so much for joining us. I know you've got to rush off now to prepare for your concert tonight. It's a tight schedule. Tomorrow you start filming *Eternally Blonde* with Heath Ledger and …

DJ   He's such a cutie, I love him to bits. And I've got a charity auction for under-privileged children in LA to fit in as well, but hey, it's cool. I can handle it.

BEN   Well, best of luck and look forward to seeing you soon.

DJ Thank you so much.

PA removes microphone wire, **DJ** *gives* **Ben** *a quick hug then disappears towards the door.* **Rod** *and* **Lola** *are waiting.*

LOLA That was great princess, and you got the bit in about the charity auction.

DJ (*to Lola*) Did my hair look all right?

LOLA Sure, I was watching the monitor, you looked fabulous, he said so! Anyway, we need to be moving to the arena now.

DJ OK, but get the people carrier round the back. I want the blue one with the darkened windows. I'm not going through the front lobby again with all that lot outside.

Scene 13: Crossing the Ruby-con

Models on catwalk. Music played in background. They walk in a determined, confident, aggressive way, with **Ruby** *in the middle constantly being buffeted and pushed from side to side. The* **models** *pose and pout at the camera while* **Ruby** *looks on anxious and bewildered.*

Models freeze. **Ruby** *gets up, looks on tentatively, moving around, studying individuals carefully, then addresses audience.*

RUBY I've seen the way they look at you. It starts with the head and works downwards, and then back up again. (*demonstrates*) Of course, this is slow motion but in reality it's done in a split second. And in that split second, they decide whether you're IN or whether you're OUT. It's as simple as that. The psychologists won't agree but let me assure you, that's the way it is. I didn't quite make it, like when you're dialling those long mobile phone numbers and you make a mistake. One digit out. That's me. 'Ruby, the Nearly Girl'. Not totally rejected, but not totally accepted either. Always redialling, always trying again, but never properly connected. And so here I am, last in the queue at the check out, and it closes just at that moment I get there – and I'm next! I shout out 'hey it's my turn now!' But it never is. They put you on hold, 'we'll bear you in mind'. You're on a reserve list, our super sub. I'm like Cinderella – the slipper never fits and I only play the first half so I never get to go to the ball. Who decides all this? They do. The 'Leaders of the Pack' (*nods towards models*) How I'd love to be her! My God, I'd die for a figure like that. She is just sooooo lucky! (*walks round one of the models*) Why can't I look like that? If only … then I could be like them, and the boys would love me. No more jokes. (*poses*) Just a little off here, and a little off there, (*motions towards hips/stomach*) that's all it takes, then I'd be like them. If only …

S c e n e   1 4 :   G i r l ' s   n i g h t   i n

*DJ's room. **Yasmin**, **Kia** and **Ruby**, looking at magazines.*

DJ Oh I just looovve that white top, that is just soooo … me.

KIA It's gorgeous, that would definitely suit you, DJ.

YASMIN Better than that top Clare Fisher was wearing on Friday night.

DJ Oh my God, that was awful.

KIA Pink sparkles … and 'I'm a babe' … I mean that is so Year 7!

DJ Clare Fisher, she's such a minger, got about as much dress sense as …

YASMIN Ruby!

RUBY Thanks! Hey are we doing this story or not?

YASMIN Clare Fisher will probably wear that top for the Leavers' Ball!

DJ We might be going to New York to get my leavers gown.

KIA New York! For your ball gown?! You're joking.

DJ No. Mum says we can do a three-day break in New York. It's not that expensive. Three days shopping and they have the most amazing fashion houses.

YASMIN You are so lucky.

DJ You know me, only the best.

YASMIN Well I only hope Russell appreciates your effort!

KIA Yeah, I heard he was taking you to the ball!

DJ In his dreams!

RUBY But I thought you said you promised him for lending you his history essay.

DJ For God's sake Ruby, you're so naïve. You didn't really think I was going to the ball with a weirdo like Russell Winter?

RUBY   You could go with him for a little while just to start off with and then, sort of, mix with your friends ...

DJ   Hello? I think I'd rather go with a ... with a hedgehog than Russell Winter!

KIA   He is so weird. Did you hear him in registration today. (*mimics*) 'Hi babycakes, do you want to make out with Russ your main man'! (*laughter*)

YASMIN   'Take a chill pill doll and cool your jets.' He freaks me out.

RUBY   I feel sorry for him. He's all right really when you get to know him.

DJ   That's something I do not want to do! Get to know him.

KIA   Unless you've got some history coursework to finish.

DJ   Yeah right!

YASMIN   I know! Why don't we ring him up?

RUBY   No!

KIA   Yeah that'll be a laugh! (*produces mobile phone*) Look, I've got his number in here somewhere. Don't ask me why.

DJ   I bet no one ever rings it.

KIA   Right ... (*starts tapping key pad*) 078356692 ... that's his ...

YASMIN   (*snatches 'phone*) Give it to me ... It's ringing! (*puts on strange accent*) Hello? Is that Russell? Oh hi! My name's Monica. (*others laugh*) I've got this friend in Year 7 and she really fancies you ... (*covers up mouthpiece she*

is laughing so much) are you still there? Her name? It's …
er … Gertrude … Gertrude Cheesyman. She's in 7R, you
must know her … but don't tell her I've called 'cos she's
really shy and she's always going on about you and
writing your name all across her maths book. And she
wants to go out with you but she daren't tell you in case
… What? You've got a girlfriend already … oh, that's a
shame … Who is it? Oh! Destiny Jade? She's your
girlfriend? Wow! That's amazing, 'cos she's like the Prom
Queen isn't she? (*laughing*) Everyone wants to go out
with her … Yeah I know, she's really pretty.

KIA   (*mimics Russ*) Oh DJ, I love you so much …

YASMIN   And you're taking her to the ball … And has
she said yes? (***DJ** pretends to stick fingers down her
throat*)

***DJ** and **Kia** sing 'He's just sk8er boy, said see you later
boy, he wasn't good enough for her …'*

YASMIN   Sshh … No it's just my radio you can hear in the
background. (*laughing*)

KIA   (*whispers*) Tell him to meet her tomorrow.

YASMIN   Can you meet her tomorrow? My friend, tell
her face to face … you know the skip, by the caretaker's
store? Gertrude wants to meet you there at break-time.
Sorry. Got to go now. Bye. (*hangs up and girls collapse
in laughter*)

YASMIN   Oh dear, he's so funny. Do you know what he
said? He goes, he goes, 'DJ's my girl but maybe I'll talk
to your friend, let her down gently … it's, like, awesome
in my presence …' He is just one weird freako!

RUBY   (*sighs*) You're so horrible you lot, and we haven't
done anything on this story.

DJ So what! Lighten up Ruby! Anyway, I'm more
interested in this play rehearsal tomorrow.

KIA Oh yeah, I might go in for that.

DJ Well step in line honey, behind the real star!

Scene 15: Busted

*The Principal's office. **Craig** sits slouched in a chair in front
of the desk waiting for **Mrs King** to arrive. When she
comes into the room he looks uneasy and apprehensive.*

70

76

93

MRS KING Well now Craig … (*sits down at her desk*)
this isn't the first time you've been in here is it?

CRAIG (*trying to put on a brave face and looking at the
floor*) Nope.

MRS KING (*looking up at **Craig***) Sit up straight when
you speak to me, young man, and look at me.

CRAIG (*a little rattled by this*) Sorry. (*he quickly sits up*)

MRS KING Now, would you like to tell me what was
going on in the corridor?

CRAIG Wasn't me, was it? I was on my way to class when …

MRS KING No, Craig. I want what actually happened.

CRAIG What's the point? You wouldn't believe me
anyway.

MRS KING Well that depends on who I'm actually
speaking to right now; is it 'Crags' the hard man of
Year 10, or Craig Burrows who I taught in Year 7 and
who can be quite a nice human being when he wants
to be? Which one are you going to be now?

CRAIG Dunno what you're talkin' about.

MRS KING So you're going to make this difficult. (*Craig looks away at the wall*) Why don't you look at me when I'm speaking to you. Craig? Do I make you nervous? Are you afraid?

CRAIG (*sounding indignant*) NO! I'm not afraid of anything.

MRS KING Yes you are, Craig. You're afraid of everything.

CRAIG (*rather less indignant now*) Dunno what ya mean.

MRS KING Will you answer me one question, Craig?

CRAIG Depends.

MRS KING Well I'll ask it anyway: how did you feel at the end of Year 7 when your father left you and your Mum?

CRAIG (*there is a pause*) Didn't bother me, did it.

MRS KING You know that's not true.

CRAIG You're not me, how'd you know how I feel?

MRS KING Because it changed everything for you, Craig. If it was me I'd have been terrified. I would have felt like the whole world had fallen apart. I would have felt that I was so insignificant I wasn't worth staying for. If that happened to me, Craig, I'd be wanting everybody to notice me, to see that I'm not weak, all because I'm afraid of being insignificant again.

CRAIG (*quieter now but still trying to sound defiant*) You don't know nothing.

MRS KING You're acting, Craig. It's a good act. Everyone believes it. The whole school thinks you're bad, you're the tough guy that nobody's going to mess with. But it's all a lie, isn't it Craig. You're not bad at all. You actually feel small, like you can be crushed.

CRAIG (*almost reluctantly*) Don't.

MRS KING Still acting, Craig. It doesn't fool me. I've got X-ray eyes, I can see through you.

CRAIG Do I get punished?

MRS KING I think this has probably been punishment enough for you. However, there is something that you're going to do for me. Since you're so good at acting I've got a little drama project that should keep you out of trouble for a while.

CRAIG (*louder now*) Acting's for girls, I'm not … (*He stops short knowing it's useless to argue.*)

MRS KING See me tomorrow morning for the details.

Craig gets up and walks to the door despondently. He turns and is about to protest once more but stops and thinks better of it. As he exits the lights fade.

S c e n e 1 6 : B e h a r d e r

Craig sitting in half-darkness holding the mirror in front of him.

CRAIG Whatta you lookin' at? You're pathetic. Pa-the-tic.

Puts mirror down and faces the audience.

Dad was hard, real hard. Hardcore. Used to say to me it was about survival, survival of the hardest. That was his lesson for life, it's what he left me, when he left me …

and my mother. He said, 'People will always want something from ya, always want to put you down, crush ya, break ya. Don't let 'em. You break *them*.' Then he was gone. We wanted too much of him. We weren't strong enough for him. I was soft back then. Cried for days. My mother said it was all right, we'd be better off. What did she know? She didn't know how to hit back, she just crumpled. Typical girl.

I'm not gonna be caught blubberin' anymore though, don't you think it. All this a bit of a revelation for you, is it? Well don't you go thinkin' you've found a way in. Nobody gets in.

'People are hard', my old man said. 'You be harder. Harder than them.' Now I've done just what me ol' Dad wanted. Anyone tries it with me an' I'll crush 'em, I'll pull 'em apart. 'Cos I'm harder. (*he looks into the mirror again*) Harder than you'll ever be.

Lights fade.

Scene 17: Perfect girl

70

73

77

Ruby sings and poses in front of mirror.

RUBY 'There's a girl in my mirror, I wonder who she is, sometimes I think I know her, sometimes I wish I really did...' Be yourself they say, just be Ruby. Be good. Be nice. Rubygood, Rubynice, Rubynormal. That's what they want. Not quite good enough. Never an A* but Ruby the good B. OK at dancing, OK at Maths, OK at life. My Mum always says 'it's nice to be important but it's more important to be nice,' but I say it's more important to be nice looking.

Moves across to stage, shuffles through magazines, sighs.

'Go for your dreams,' that's what DJ told me, it's easy to say that when you look like a Hollywood Princess. (*picks up mobile phone, looks at magazine and dials*)

VOICE-OVER (*off stage*) Hi, who's calling the Perfect Girl Line?

RUBY It's Ruby here and I want to be like them ... (*pointing to models in magazine*)

VOICE (*interrupting*) Listen carefully to all your options.

Catwalk models return to stage, crossing in front of Ruby, beside and behind her – background music played – models speak.

MODEL 1 If you require a super-flat stomach, press one.

MODEL 2 For celeb looks and makeover, press two.

MODEL 3 For thin legs that look great in jeans, press three.

MODEL 4 How to be a flirt with the boys, press four.

MODEL 1 How to have bags of confidence and not bags under your eyes, press five.

MODEL 2 For a nice tight bum, press six.

MODEL 3 For fantastic cleavage, press seven.

MODEL 4 If you wanna have super-sexy looks and more fun, go blonde and press eight.

Ruby desperately trying to key in her numbers but getting confused and frustrated (this sequence with models can be repeated). Voice comes back on line, models exit.

VOICE-OVER Thank you for calling Perfect Girl and now here's today recipe.

*Enter **Phil**, dressed in apron with mixing bowl. He uses the table nearby with bottle and ingredients on it. He speaks with a Cockney accent. **Ruby** looks on, confused and clutching her phone. Then she notices **Phil**.*

PHIL And so today my friends, we are going to attempt to create the perfect female. So first up you're gonna need a little fat, not too much fat, we're talking female here (*laughs*). Say enough from seven bars of soap. Or you can use the bottled variety like I've done (*pours fat into container*) then enough iron from one nail (*displays and throws in nail*), about eight spoons full of sugar, gotta keep the little ladies nice and sweet, a little bit of lime, stir in nicely, cup full of salt, garnish with a bit of potash and sulphur – several thousand matches will do … finally loads and loads of water, mix it all together … there you go … and you just pop that in the oven, temperature's gotta be just right, that's 98.4°F … leave for about two thousand years and you should get it just about right … the perfect female … And here's one we made earlier. (*walks over and gestures towards table, figure of **DJ** rises, smile on her face*)

DJ (*saunters towards front of stage, slow walk*)
I have hair swept into a timeless crown of gold
And lips that lock in a curvy smile
You could be my friend awhile
All those pubs and clubs to see
On my slender arm you'll be
Trailing with your plain old face
Come on! Step it up a pace.
It's DJ here, the Chosen One
Created just to have some fun
Shopping sprees and all alike
Hit the town, good times tonight
All the boys shall come to me
But maybe one for you, we'll see

And then next week I shall go again
(*moving in between models and links arms*)
Becky! Rachel! Are you free too?
Oh yes, DJ! We are for you! (*models speak with **DJ***)
(***DJ** and models freeze*)*

PHIL There you go, perfect! What did I tell you!

RUBY But I'm not am I? (*crossly*)

PHIL What?

RUBY Perfect. You didn't make me like them. (*nods towards **DJ** and models*)

PHIL Listen darling, I just do the basic ingredients ... I made you perfect inside … it's up to you what you do with the rest ... if it ain't broken, don't mend it!

*Exit **Phil** and models. **Ruby** sighs and sits down, magazines at feet, looking fed up. Fade out lights.*

* DJ Poem *written by Natasha Malcolm-Brown (aged 15)*

Scene 18: The school hall

*The school stage: onstage are **DJ**, **Yasmin**, **Ruby** and **Russell**. DJ and **Yasmin** are preening themselves, **Russell** is trying to get **DJ** to notice him by walking around her in a conspicuous manner (but pretending to be inconspicuous) and 'playing it cool'. **Ruby** sits by herself at the table.*

RUBY Er, excuse me, can we … er, get started. We've got a lot to do.

Everyone ignores her and she sits back exasperated.

DJ Okay, we can start now that I've decided what I'm wearing.

Everyone walks to the table following DJ.

DJ Look, I've got the whole thing planned out. *(she takes out some papers from her folder and shows the costume designs she has made to the others)*

DJ I've decided on this rather chic little silver top that I got from 'Perfect Girl' together with these flared jeans.

YASMIN That's perfect DJ. You mean the jeans with the embroidered bottoms?

DJ Of course.

RUSSELL *(looking at DJ, besotted)* Then you will truly be … a princess.

RUBY But … but we haven't sorted the parts out yet … have we?

YASMIN Oh come on. It's obvious that DJ has got to play the princess. *(looking at Ruby)* I mean, who else is there? *(DJ looks smug)*

RUSSELL *(still besotted)* Then you will truly be … a princess.

RUBY Well, actually we've already got the costume for the princess from last year.

She goes to the prop box and pulls out a more traditional fairy-tale princess costume. DJ and Yasmin look horrified.

DJ You must be joking! I'm not wearing those stupid little white socks, and that skirt, I mean, pleeeease!

At that moment Mr Lucas walks in with Craig, who looks like he doesn't want to be there.

MR LUCAS Hello you lot. Oh, DJ, I see you're the

princess. The perfect choice. (**DJ** *looks smugly at* **Ruby** *who sits back exasperated again*) Just as well because I've brought Prince Charming here for you. (*he brings* **Craig** *to the table*)

CRAIG I'm not playing that! That's gay that is.

RUSSELL (*to* **DJ**, *still besotted*) I will be your prince.

CRAIG Yeah, let him do it.

DJ Why do we have to have him?!

KIA Yeah, why do we have to have him?

MR LUCAS I'm afraid you're going to have to take this up with Mrs King. Orders from the top you see; Craig has got to do his community service. Isn't that right Craig, my boy.

CRAIG I'm not your boy.

DJ Aw, pleeeeease Mr Lucas. You know you love me really. (*she flutters her eye lids at him*)

MR LUCAS Sorry DJ. It's out of my hands. Anyway, he can play the wolf, can't he Ruby?

RUBY But we're doing Snow White!

MR LUCAS Well, improvise. That's what drama's all about. Goodbye.

Mr Lucas exits hastily.

CRAIG Yeah, I'm the wolf.

RUBY But there isn't a wolf in this play.

CRAIG There is now 'cos I'm playing him. Mr Lucas said. I'm the wolf.

RUSSELL I'm the prince and you (*to DJ*) are my ...

DJ I'm the princess ...

RUBY But who's going to play the ugly, wicked step-mother?

She looks up and everyone is looking at her.

RUBY What?

DJ You're perfect for that. That part's made for you.

RUBY But ...

DJ (*interrupting* **Ruby**) After all, we're only acting, aren't we? (*she winks at* **Yasmin**).

RUBY But ...

DJ (*interrupting*) Now, I've got the whole thing planned out.

Lights fade.

Scene 19: Reflections

Russell is in his bedroom. He has a full-length mirror set up in front of him leaning against a chair. He is posing in front of it, experimenting with different versions of 'cool'.

RUSSELL (*posing and with American accent*) Yo Destiny, my main girl! What's happenin' in the hood?! How about you and me go lay down some smooth, groovy tracks at my pad?

He stops and reconsiders, then strikes a new pose, the 'tough guy', and speaks with a gravely Clint Eastwood-type voice.

Just watch it, punk. Don't make me angry. You wouldn't like me when I'm angry. (*coming out of pose and character*) I don't know, it's not quite right. Maybe it should be more like … (*striking an easy pose, hands in pockets and speaking in a Michael Caine-type Cockney accent*) Now maybe you didn't 'ear me the first time. If you're looking for some barney rubble – that's trouble – you just carry on sunshine.

Suddenly a strange noise fills the room. **Russell** *looks around, perplexed and frightened. A figure steps out of the mirror – it is his reflection.* **Russell** *picks up a stool and holds it above him ready to strike.*

RUSSELL II   Whoa! Whoa! Russ, ol' buddy, ol' pal. Look who it is.

RUSSELL   Who … who are you? How did you get in here?

RUSSELL II   OK, just take it easy with the upraised weapon. Look at me. Don't I look familiar? Notice a slight resemblance, maybe?

Russell looks closely. He raises his arms and the reflection does the same thing. Whatever action Russell does the reflection copies.

RUSSELL   But … but … you're me. (*panics*) Oh no, I've been sucked into a parallel dimension where everyone looks like me! I knew this would happen one day!

RUSSELL II   Whoa, Russ. Just calm down. It's OK, I'm just your reflection. You see me every day and I, unfortunately, have got to see you.

RUSSELL   My reflection? How is that possible?

RUSSELL II   Look, just play along. It's just a cheap, gimmicky plot device put in by the writer to get the play going. It's kinda sagging at the moment.

Russell They can do that?

Russell II Okay, I've got to make this quick, I haven't much time left before I must return. Now you just sit on that stool and LISTEN. (*Russ sits down*) Now I watch you every day, morning, noon and night going up to that mirror over there and doing your thing.

Russell So what do you think I should...?

Russell II (*interrupting him*) Russ, it's better for you to just listen now, okay? Let me do the talking. Now what I see is tragic. It's sad. It's ... it's humiliating. I see a perfectly good bloke making an idiot of himself, in his bedroom, at least three times a day. It's sad, sad, sad.

Russell But I think I've almost got it – I've nearly unlocked the secret to 'cool', then I can make my move on Destiny Jade and sweep her off her feet. I think I'm starting to look good.

Russell II Oh dear, oh dear. We are in BIG trouble, aren't we? I knew there'd be a girl involved in this somewhere. Look Russ, time is short so I'll cut to the chase: all of this is just acting – it's not you. People aren't stupid, they can see an actor a million miles away, they can spot a fake, and you my friend are so tragically FAKE. Look, just don't try so hard. Believe me, and take it from a self-respecting reflection who knows, 'what you see is not always what you get, so just give them who you are'. Right, my time is up. Good luck, Russ.

Russell Wait, what do you mean? Don't go ...

Russell II Russ, try not to be so ... how shall I put it ... so pathetic. Figure it out, listen to what I said. And by the way, I'd think about why you've got to try so hard to impress that girl. Anyway, gotta go. Bye!

There is the strange sound again and the reflection disappears back into the mirror. **Russell** *walks over to the mirror and looks behind it and around it to check if the reflection is still there. He then looks into it intently.*

RUSSELL   'What you see isn't always what you get'. Hmmm. 'Give them who you are'? I've got a funny feeling about this.

Scene 20: Anything but ordinary

Models on stage, posing. They all wear large labels, stuck on, or hanging round necks ... Fantastic ... Wow factor ... Fab ... **Ruby** *appears, she is wearing large labels ... Ordinary ... average ... OK ... The models appear to be surrounded by an invisible force field and* **Ruby** *can't get amongst them.*

RUBY   (*to audience*) I can't do it. I can't break in, however hard I try. They won't let me. So that's it I suppose. Little Miss Ordinary. But I don't want to be ordinary! You're not listening out there, anything but ordinary! (*optional: end scene with music or dance, for example 'Anything but Ordinary' by Avril Lavigne*)

Scene 21: Falling

Lunchtime, the playground. **DJ** *is the centre of attention with* **Yasmin**, **Kia** *and a few other girls. They are boy spotting.*

YASMIN   So who's it going to be?

DJ   You just can't rush this kind of thing. Who you're seen going to the Leavers' Ball with is one of the most important decisions you have to make in life. It goes with your first modelling/TV/film contract and the first face-lift, not that I'll ever need one of those!

Several boys go by. The girls smile, then make 'puking' actions and roll their eyes.

YASMIN   (*pointing at different boys*) Too fat! Too thin! Too stupid! Yuck, too ugly! When will the right guy ever turn up.

*Enter **Russell**. **Yasmin** sees him and quickly turns to **DJ**.*

YASMIN   Uh oh! Freaky weirdo boy at three'o'clock!

DJ   Quick! Hide me!

*The girls stand in front of **DJ** blocking her from **Russell's** view. He approaches the girls with a bit of a swagger.*

RUSSELL   You girls all right? (*He then notices **DJ** and loses some of his composure*) Oh, DJ. I, er, didn't see you there. I was … I was … er, wondering, could I, er, talk to you?

DJ   You go right ahead, Russell. (*all the girls gather in more closely unnerving **Russell***)

RUSSELL   Er, just call me Russ. I, er, wonder if we could, maybe, have a private conversation?

DJ   But, Russ, of course. (*to the girls*) It's alright, he's a friend. I'll see you later.

*The girls move a little further off but within hearing distance. They watch **Russell** like hawks.*

DJ   Now, Russ, what would you like to talk about?

RUSSELL   Now that we're alone I'd just like to say how

lovely you're looking today.

DJ (*looking puzzled, wondering where this is going*)
Yesssss?

RUSSELL (*a bit panicked*) Oh, er, but of course I don't
just mean *today*. You look radical, NO! I mean *radiant*,
yes, you look radiant, every day, all the time, three
hundred and sixty-five days a year … (***DJ** looks at him
pitifully*) … except on a leap year … of course. (*the girls
behind are sniggering and **Russell** looks forlorn*) I think
I've got a headache.

DJ That's just sooooo sweet Russ. Is that what you
wanted to say to me?

RUSSELL Well yes … and no. I was, er, wondering about
the ball. Now there have been some … well, ugly and
frankly scurrilous rumours about, that you are still
looking for someone to go to the ball with.

DJ (*with mock surprise*) NO!

RUSSELL YES!

DJ (*still mocking*) Don't you worry Russ. You're the only
man for me. (*the girls behind start giggling – **Russ**
looks a little disconcerted by this*)

RUSSELL So … so they are just rumours?

DJ Of course, Russ.

RUSSELL (*still unsure*) And you're still going to the ball
with me?

DJ Of course, Russ. Who else could I possibly want to go
with?

At that moment a couple of good-looking blokes walk

*past. They smile at **DJ** and she smiles and waves at them flirtatiously. **Russell** looks outraged, then crestfallen. The girls behind start giggling again.*

DJ   Oh, sorry. Where were we?

Russell   (*looking pitiful*) Nowhere …

DJ   Russ, sweetie, I've got to go. People to see, things to do, you know.

Russell   Yup.

DJ   Ciao, sweetie. (*she blows him a kiss in a mocking manner then turns*) Ooh guys!

*DJ exits after the boys. The girls follow her, but not before having one last giggling fit at **Russell's** expense.*

Russell   (*still crestfallen*) 'What you see isn't always what you get'. I think I get it now. That was humiliating.

Lights fade.

Scene 22: Mirror, mirror

*One of the extras comes onto the stage holding big poster saying: 'The big day. The play's the thing. A new version of Snow White written by Year 10, with a little help from Mr Lucas.' **Dopey (Ant)**, **Sleepy (Roy)** and the **wolf (Craig)** come on stage and face the audience.*

Dopey   Once upon a time …

Sleepy   There was a beautiful princess called Snow White …

*Both look at the **wolf**, waiting for him to come up with the next line. Awkward silence. **Sleepy** nudges the **wolf**.*

WOLF Get off ... (*Wolf shoves **Sleepy** into **Dopey**, then he looks at the audience*) And there was her ugly old cow of a stepmother. Right, that's it, I've had enough of this poncey play.

*Craig walks off. Enter wicked **step-mother** (**Ruby** dressed in well padded costume), carrying a rosy apple. She passes the two **dwarves**.*

DOPEY Don't know about no rosy apple but she looks like a dried up old prune.

SLEEPY Yeah, but have you seen her step-daughter, Snow White? She's one fit bird.

DOPEY In your dreams!

*Exit **dwarves**. **Step-mother** tuts. **Snow White** enters. (DJ) She is dressed in casual trendy clothes.*

STEP-MOTHER Mirror Mirror on the Wall who is the fairest of them all ...? (*looking in mirror*)

SNOW WHITE (*DJ*) Well obviously not you, and I'm not falling for this old trick either. (*snatches apple and throws it away*) Haven't you got any Diet Coke?

STEP-MOTHER It's no good, Snow White, they all think I'm ugly.

SNOW WHITE (*speaking in American accent, Hollywood style*) Nonsense, to me Step-Mummy you're just like an oil painting.

STEP-MOTHER Oh, do you mean because I look like the beautiful Mona Lisa, painted in oils?

SNOW WHITE No, because your hair's streaky, your skin's oily and you smell like an old banger.

STEP-MOTHER   I'm sorry Snow White, I just want to be as beautiful as you.

SNOW WHITE   Excuse me? I don't think so.

STEP-MOTHER   But I look in the mirror every day and I hate myself. Is there nothing that can be done? (*picks up mirror*)

SNOW WHITE   Well … I suppose we could give you a makeover. (*whistles*) Boys! We gotta customer.

*Enter **dwarves** who push **step-mother** on the table and start prodding her about.*

DOPEY   Oh dear, we shall have to do something about these roots.

SLEEPY   And look at these laughter lines …

GRUMPY   And them crow's feet make her look ten years older.

DOPEY   And she'll need a tummy tuck … (*prodding tummy*)

STEP-MOTHER   Ouch!

GRUMPY   And liposuction, get rid of all this ugly fat.

DOPEY   Just cut her head off then, that should do the trick.

SLEEPY   Don't forget the nose, needs at least an inch off the end, broken and reshaped, it won't hurt too much.

STEP-MOTHER   What!

SLEEPY   And what about a boob job? That should make a lot of difference.

STEP-MOTHER   Oh no no no no … no you don't. I draw the line at that, I don't need a boob job.

SLEEPY   Course you do, everyone's having it done these days.

STEP-MOTHER   Yeah, I've heard about them, they might swell up and burst and I don't want an empty boob tube.

GRUMPY   Stop worrying big momma and just relax, a little anaesthetic is all we need.

STEP-MOTHER   Help!! (***Step-mother*** *is carried away*)

SNOW WHITE   (*looking at* ***Dopey***) I find ugliness such a barrier to communication.

DOPEY   Yeah, she is a bit ugly. (*nodding towards* ***Step-mother***)

SNOW WHITE   I meant you, Dork features. Anyway, I've got a photo shoot in the forest with Prince Charming. You can't imagine what it's like to be a supermodel, everyone wants a piece of you.

Snow White *flounces off stage. Enter* ***Dopey***.

DOPEY   Later that day in the enchanted forest.

Exit ***Dopey***, *enter* ***Prince Charming (Russ)***.

PRINCE   (*speaking in deep heroic voice to audience*) I am the fearless and incredibly good-looking Prince Charming.

Craig, *the* ***wolf***, *walks on stage behind* ***Russell*** *and taps him on the shoulder.*

WOLF   Oi! Am I on yet?

Russell turns round and screams in shock then quickly recovers.

PRINCE (*hushed tone to Craig*) No, no, get off this is my big scene.

Wolf growls at Prince who jumps. Wolf exits. Prince turns to audience again, composing himself.

PRINCE I am here to meet the beautiful, the divine Princess Snow White and I will protect her in this deep, dark forest.

Enter Snow White, noisily talking on her mobile phone, making the Prince jump. Snow White is accompanied by her PA (Yasmin) carrying clipboard.

SNOW WHITE Sorry, no can do sweety, got my photoshoot now ... We'll do lunch another day, must go darling, ciao. (*gives phone to Yasmin*) Hold all my calls.

PRINCE My dearest darling Princess, do not fear, I will protect you.

SNOW WHITE Oh princy poo, I'm just like sooo busy right now, do you mind awfully much if we get on with the pictures?

PRINCE No problem, my angel. (*Prince snaps fingers*) Come on everybody! Lights, music, camera, action! (*loud pop music starts, spotlight on Snow White, as she poses and pouts dramatically like a model. Prince is seen taking photos*)

PRINCE (*instructions*) Come on baby, give me sexy, that's it! (*taking photos*) Wonderful darling, wonderful, you're a star! (*lights and music fade*)

SNOW WHITE Oh I'm sooo exhausted darling, being perfect is such hard work!

Step-mother enters. She has changed. Her make-up is overly done and garish, huge 'bust' which has clearly been padded out and deliberately over exaggerated.

STEP-MOTHER   (*looking uncomfortable*) Well, what do you think?

PRINCE   (*looking shocked*) Ruby … I mean step-mum, what have you done?

SNOW WHITE   Oh my God! Oh my God! Is it really you?

STEP-MOTHER   Now Snow White, I can be as beautiful as you and everyone will think we're sisters. I am so happy!

SNOW WHITE   She's attractive I suppose, but I wouldn't exactly call her beautiful. Her eyes are too close together for a start, her hair's dyed, it's not soft and natural like mine. And her bum's still too big. (*DJ walks round her pointing out imperfections*) She'll never be as perfect as me.

*Snaps her fingers and **dwarves** walk on with the mirror. **Snow White** starts posing again.*

SNOW WHITE   I have style, sophistication, elegance and grace, things you know nothing about, loser!

STEP-MOTHER   But … I've had a full makeover ...

SNOW WHITE   Listen Ruby … oh, I mean mumsy, you will never have what I've got. You're plain and boring, that's what you'll always be!

PA   (**Yasmin** *whispers to* **Snow White**) Hold on DJ, that isn't in the script.

SNOW WHITE   I'm King Girl around here in case you haven't noticed. I've got the perfect figure, the perfect hair, the perfect nails. Don't you just wish you were me Ruby?

PRINCE   (*whispering to DJ*) What are you saying? This isn't in the play.

Ruby pushes past Russell – Ruby angrily pulls off wig and fake padding for her bust, and uses it to wipe off make-up.

DJ   (*to Ruby*) What are you doing? This is my big scene!

RUBY   You're right about one thing DJ, I'll never be like you. You might be beautiful on the outside but you're ugly inside.

DJ   (*looks shocked*) How dare you speak to me like that? (*puts on tearful appearance, pretends to sob and appeals to Prince*) Are you just going to stand there and let her get away with that?

RUSSELL   Ruby's right, she'll never be like you and I'm glad about that.

Ruby throws wig and materials at DJ who catches them. Ruby walks off stage confidently, Russell follows behind. DJ looks at Yasmin and the dwarves. Yasmin looks on apologetically but still walks away with the other cast members. Leaving DJ centre stage by herself. DJ stops pretending to cry and looks at audience and sneers.

DJ   I don't need them anyway.

She tosses her head, pouts and storms off stage. Enter Craig still dressed as the wolf.

WOLF   Am I on yet? (*curtain quickly falls*)

Scene 23: Unbreakable

70

The lights come up from the previous scene. **Craig** *enters still in his wolf outfit and sits facing the audience. There is a spotlight on him.*

CRAIG Been taught a lesson 'aven't I? Bad Craig, put him in a play, that'll make him look stupid. Come on, what you waiting for? Let's have a big laugh about that! That'll teach 'im. That'll break 'im. No way. Not this boy. He's unbreakable. It's the only way to be when you've been broken before. Yeah, that's right, I've been broken before. Smashed to pieces. Ground into dust. Then left to blow away in the wind. When your own Dad leaves you, that's what you feel – like nothing, like dust. All you've got is pieces of yourself lying all over the place. It gets messy. It needs to be cleared up. Everyday, I'm clearing myself up, getting all the pieces in place, putting together a me that isn't going to break again. So, one lousy play, all them lousy teachers and them poncey kids can't touch me. I've got nothing to lose 'cos I've lost everything. Self-preservation. Self-destruction. It's all the same to me. No-one gets through. No-one comes near. Got a problem with that, sunshine?

Lights fade.

Scene 24: Maybe

76

The school playground. The bell goes and there is the sound of children. **Russell** *enters looking forlorn. He slumps down and takes out his lunch.* **Ruby** *then enters. They both notice each other, there is an awkward moment where they are not sure what to say or do.* **Ruby** *starts to walk away then stops and approaches* **Russell**.

He gets up.

RUSS (*slightly nervously*) Would you, er, like a crisp?

RUBY No, no. I don't eat. I … I mean I don't feel hungry. (**Russell** *looks at her and she looks away momentarily*) OK, just one. (*she reaches into the packet*) Might as well, I didn't have any breakfast.

RUSS It was a bit of a disaster last night wasn't it?

RUBY (*looking ashamed*) I'm sorry.

RUSS What? What for?

RUBY I'm sorry that I ruined it for everybody.

RUSS No, no! I didn't mean that. You didn't ruin anything. I meant … I mean …

RUBY I feel humiliated. I embarrassed everyone.

RUSS Wait a minute, the play was brilliant, the audience loved it. Really. Mr. Lucas said it was the funniest version of Snow White he'd ever seen.

RUBY DJ and her friends aren't talking to me. I think they've been talking about me behind my back.

RUSS You've got to ignore her, forget about her. She's … she's not what I thought at first.

RUBY I thought you and DJ were going to the ball together.

RUSS Yeah, well, that isn't happening anymore. Look, I was stupid. I got caught up believing she was perfect, but she wasn't what she seemed and I was too blind to see it. If it hadn't been for last night I would still be making a fool of myself.

Ruby Well, actually, you have been a bit of a prat.

Russ Thanks.

Ruby But I like you better now.

Russ (*surprised*) Really! (*reconsidering*) Er, what do you mean?

Ruby Well, you seem more … well … more like yourself.

Russ And … and you like that?

Ruby Well, yeah. Why not?

Russ Because, er, because, well …

Ruby Russ, you're babbling.

Russ (*nervous*) Sorry. Er, I was thinking, since I don't have a date for the ball, I was wondering if … if …

Ruby Yes?

Russ (*very nervous*) … If you would, you know, er, if you didn't mind, maybe, perhaps, possibly you'd like to come with, er, you know … me.

Ruby No.

Russ Huh?

Ruby Well … maybe.

Russ Maybe as in 'yes, I would very much like to accompany you', or maybe as in 'this is a nice way of saying no'?

Ruby (*smiling and Russ smiles back*) Just maybe. (*she turns to go*)

RUSS I'll call you … (when **Ruby** is some distance away]
   YESSSSSS!!

*Disco music starts. **Russell** starts dancing and gyrating like
John Travolta. Starts singing 'Ooh ooh ooh ooh staying
alive, staying alive, ooh ooh ooh ooh going to the ball,
going to the ball'.*

RUBY Russ! (*the music stops abruptly and **Russ** freezes
   in the famous John Travolta pose – as **Ruby** walks
   towards him he pretends he is scratching his armpit and
   Ruby gives him a stern look*) Russ!

RUSS (*becoming himself again*) Sorry.

RUBY (*smiling*) I did only say maybe.

They begin walking off together.

RUSS I know, I know …

Lights fade. Disco music plays out.

BEFORE YOU BEGIN WORK ON THE PLAY

Before working on a play, the director and actors have to be clear about the **themes and issues** it raises. The director and actors will also need to have insight into the **characters**. *Face Value* revolves around four main characters: Russ, DJ, Craig, Ruby.

Activities

1 Working in a small group, decide what you think are the main themes/issues in *Face Value* using the list below. Try to put them into a rank order with the most important first, though it may be difficult to decide exactly which single theme is the most important:

School life, Image, Being famous, Bullying, Self-esteem, Friendship, Male/Female stereotypes, Embarrassment

2 In your group, take the theme/issue at the top of your list and make a spider diagram, brainstorming any words or ideas associated with that theme.

3 As a class, discuss why it is important to study these themes/issues. Consider how they are relevant to you.

4 Work in pairs. **Russ** is always acting a part and trying on a variety of different roles. Remind yourselves what they are by looking at Scenes 1, 4, 5, 6, 18 and 19 (pages, 6, 11, 14, 15, 49, 52).

5 Now draw a picture of Russ, but try to put in clues about the different roles he plays. For example, he may be holding a high-tech spy gadget for his role as 'Brad Wolf' the super-spy. You could divide the picture in half down the middle: one side could be the real Russ and the other could be the parts he plays.

6 In your pairs, discuss why you think Russ is always playing a part and is rarely himself. Reading Scene 5 may give you some clues (page 14).

7 **DJ** is a character of contrasts – between the image she has of herself and the reality of what she is like. Work out

what these contrasts are by reading Scenes 3, 12, 18 and 22 (pages 10, 32, 49, 58).

8 Discuss how DJ sees herself and the way she sees and treats other people, particularly Russ and Ruby.

9 **Craig** has a single image that remains the same throughout the play. Remind yourself of what it is by reading Scenes 4 and 6 (pages 11 and 15).

10 Discuss why you think Craig behaves and acts this way. Scene 15 and 23 may give you some clues (pages 43 and 65). Is there another side to Craig?

11 **Ruby** is a character with low self-esteem. In your pair, make a list of the things that worry her and affect the way she sees herself. Look at Scenes 10, 13, 17 and 20 (pages 27, 38, 46, 55).

STAGECRAFT

Plays are essentially written to be performed to an audience. This means that the director and actors have to make the words and action on the page come alive. They would also have to interpret how to make a scene work, as the script gives plenty of clues but not all of the answers.

The director

As the director of a play or scene, you have overall responsibility for the success of the performance. Your main concern is the actors and their performance. However, you also have to consider other things like costume, stage design, lighting and music.

Activities

1 Re-read Scene 6, so you know what happens (page 15).

2 Working in a group of five, nominate one director and devise three **still-life pictures** that show key moments in the scene (possibly one from the beginning, middle and end).

- The director will have to assign roles to each of the actors.

- When putting the actors in place, the director must decide how to maximise the use of the performance space. If everyone is too close together everything will seem crammed and the audience's view may be obscured by some actors blocking out others. If they are too far apart the audience may miss the central focus of the scene.

- You may initially want to draw a rough plan of how to position the actors using a bird's eye view.

- When the actors are in place, work out what pose and facial expression they should have.

- Make sure that the three still-life pictures show how the events of the scene have progressed.

3 Now allow the actors to improvise their roles. Start with the first still life from the last activity. Begin with a 'freeze', but when the director says 'action' the actors should perform *without using any words* – they must communicate how they feel through actions, body language and facial expressions.

4 Experiment with the improvisations from the last activity and offer alternatives for how to play the parts. Try the following for the girls in the class:

- They could be disgusted with Russ's behaviour.

- They could be amused by it.

- They could be 'freaked out' by it.

- They could behave threateningly toward him.

- Try a combination of these.

- Think about how Russ would react to each of these situations.

5 Once you have established the movement and action of the scene, allow the actors to perform their lines. Again, consider experimenting with different ways of presenting each one. Take, for example, Mrs Hayes' line to Russ:

'Your future, young man, is looking *very* uncertain from where I'm standing. *(shouting)* NOW GET OUT OF MY CLASS!'

How would she say the first half of the line? Calmly?
Threateningly? Sarcastically?

Stage properties

Apart from the acting, there are other practical problems that a
director must overcome.

The **set design** can pose potential problems, particularly if you
have a very small budget. The clue is to have a few objects
which *suggest* the setting without having to recreate the whole
thing. For example, rather than rebuild a school canteen in its
entirety you could instead use two school desks placed end to
end with a paper table cloth over them; you could have school
chairs next to the table and perhaps a litter bin; on the table
there could be food wrappers, plastic cups, plastic plates and
some cutlery.

Props should be used in the same way as the set – you only
need enough to *suggest* the scene. However, there may be
occasions when a scene absolutely requires a prop because of a
particular effect that needs to be created.

Music and **sound** effects are a useful tool to help convey a
scene. Music and songs can also be used symbolically to reflect
something about the characters or the themes or events in a
scene. For example, to introduce and end Craig's monologues
(Scene 8, page 21 and Scene 16, page 45) some heavy rock
music could be used, or even an appropriate rap track.

Activities

6   Think about what basic elements could be used to suggest
    the following settings from the play:

    ■ a classroom (Scene 6, page 16 and Scene 9, page 22)

    ■ the staff room (Scene 11, page 30)

    ■ celebrity dressing room (Scene 12, page 34)

    ■ fairy-tale set (Scene 22, page 61)

7   Re-read Scene 19, page 52, where Russ's reflection comes
    out of the mirror and begins talking to him.

- As a director this poses a challenge – how do you allow the audience to see the reflection actually coming out of the mirror?

- Consider how you would design the mirror for this scene to work. There are some practical problems you would have to overcome: how can it be made stable enough for an actor to come through it? How can the actor come through the mirror? What material might you use instead of the normal mirror glass? How can it be made light and easy enough to carry?

- Draw a sketch with labels on to illustrate your design.

8 With a partner, brainstorm songs or pieces of music which relate to the following themes of the play:

identity/image; celebrity; boys and girls; acting/pretending.

9 Re-read Scene 17, page 46. With a partner decide the following:

- What music you would use through the scene? How would this change with the different events and characters?

- Where would you start, pause, lower the volume, raise the volume and stop the music?

10 Using sound effects wisely can set the scene and save you having to recreate everything using setting and props. Look at the following scenes and decide what sounds effects would be useful in conveying the setting:

- school playground (Scene 4, page 11)

- school corridor (Scene 2, page 8, and Scene 7, page 18)

- canteen (Scene 10, page 27)

11 In a small group, consider how you would put on Scene 1 by coming up with ideas for set design, props, music and sound effects. Use sketches and bird's eye view plans with labels to help you.

12 As directors, how would your group choreograph the opening of the scene till just before Anthony enters?

Y7: S&L16-19; Y8: S&L14-16; Y9: S&L11, 12

DRAMA EXPLORATION

Character acting

As an actor, playing a role means *becoming* that character; a successful performance means convincing the audience that you really are the person you are playing. There are some basic things to consider when playing a character:

- **Voice**. How would that character speak? Is their voice deep, light, heavy, etc? Do they speak quickly, slowly, confidently, softly? Do they have an accent? How might they speak differently in different situations or with other characters?

- **Movement**. How would your character move about the performance space? Would they move quickly, slowly, swiftly, clumsily? Is this a character with lots of movement or does he/she stay quite still? How would your character move in different situations?

- **Body (posture)**. How would you stand and hold yourself to tell the audience something about your character? Will your character be slouched, standing upright, relaxed, stiff, heavy?

- **Mannerisms**. Is there a particular speech pattern, movement or gesture that defines your character – for example, flicking hair, frantic hand movements, hands in pockets, particular words/phrases?

Remember that all these elements should be used together to reflect the character you are playing.

Activities

1 To practise using voice to bring your character to life look at these examples, which involve three of the main characters:

- DJ: Oh my GOD! It was like sooooooo embarrassing! You should have *seen* what she was wearing!

- CRAIG: Now take a look at the lot of ya. Soft, that's what you are, soft. Pathetic. And what do you think you're looking at?

- RUBY: Why can't I look like that? If only … then I could be like them, and the boys would love me.

Each of these examples provides clues for how to play the character. Attempt reading each one aloud and try to show the differences between the characters by using some of the suggestions from the voice tips above.

2 Now read two examples from Russ:

- RUSSELL: The problem, if you want to know, is ME. Yup, me. Good ol' Russell Winter. The name just about says it all…

- RUSSELL: Hey, take a chill pill, girl! Just cool your jets and let ol' daddy here know what's going down, what's the buzz, what's the scene … baby … cakes!

Because Russ is always playing different roles you will need to have a range of vocal styles to use for him depending on what part he is playing. Try speaking the two examples above and attempt to show a difference in the way he would speak.

3 Try experimenting with **movement** and **posture**. In a small group, move around the performance space using the following cues:

- move as if you are heavy
- move as if you are a model
- move with a purpose in a confident manner
- move as if you are very small/very big.

4 Now, in your group, select one of the main characters each. One by one, begin with a standing pose then walk across the performance space as you imagine your character might.

5 Try taking one of the lines for your character from Activity 1 and move and speak in character. The others in the group can act as directors and offer practical suggestions to help you improve your performance.

Y7: S&L15,17; Y8: S&L14,15

Character development

Characters very often change in the audience's eyes throughout the course of a play.

- The character may actually learn and change during the course of the play.

- The character may behave differently in changing circumstances, so the audience's perception of the character develops.

- The character's motives and intentions may be gradually revealed to the audience so we have a better understanding of them.

- Occasionally, a central character *doesn't* show any development and stays the same throughout the play. If this is the case, the actor has to consider the reasons why the writer has portrayed the character in this way.

Activities

6 Among the main characters in *Face Value*, some develop more than others. With a partner, work out which of the main characters you think show some development using the bullet-points above. Look at the following scenes to help you:

- RUSS: Scene 1, page 6; Scene 6, page 15; Scene 19, page 52 and Scene 24, page 65.

- CRAIG: Scene 8, page 21; Scene 15, page 43; Scene 22, page 58.

- DJ: Scene 3, page 9; Scene 10, page 27; Scene 12, page 32 and Scene 21, page 55.

- RUBY: Scene 2, page 8; Scene 13, page 38; Scene 20, page 55 and Scene 24, page 65.

7 Discuss. Which character doesn't actually change much but develops the most in the audience's eyes? Why do you think this is? What might the writers have been trying to show by doing this?

8 Which character by the end has changed the most?

9 A good actor should be able to show an audience how a character develops through the course of the play.

Working in a small group, choose one of the main characters and decide how you can show that character's development. Divide the group into two actors and two directors:

■ Begin with a simple still life, one from the beginning of the play and another from the end.

■ Think about how you would use **posture** and **facial expressions** to show the difference in your main character.

■ Now take a significant line to add to your two still images. Decide how the actor's **voice** could be used to show the change in the character.

■ Add some **movement** to the images. How might the character move differently in the later scene to the earlier one? Is s/he more or less confident? Does s/he make bigger or smaller movements? Do they move more quickly or more slowly?

 10 Imagine that you can project the characters of DJ, Craig, Russell and Ruby 15 years into the future when they will be around 30 years old. Choosing either a 'magazine' style format or a paragraph, write a short piece about what you think has happened to each character. You may wish to include details of their education, home, partners, children, employment, hobbies, achievements, main events. When you are finished, turn to the back of this book to see how the authors think the characters will develop.

11 In what ways has Ruby's character changed by the end of the play? Discuss in small groups.

 12 In Scene 17, page 46, Ruby is confronted in her imagination by the magazine models she so desperately yearns to be like. Imagine you are the editor of a problem page in a teenage magazine, what advice would you give to Ruby?

 13 Find out! Scene 13, page 38, is called 'Crossing the Ruby-con'. The original Crossing of the Rubicon took place hundreds of years ago and involved a river and a famous person. Who was that person and what was significant about that event? Why do you think the authors have used the expression 'Crossing the Rubycon' in connection with Ruby?

The subtext and symbolism

A skilled director would look beyond the obvious events of a scene and 'read between the lines', looking for any hidden meanings and ideas and considering how these fit in with the main themes/issues. This is known as reading the subtext. Sometimes these 'hidden' meanings are built into the structure of a scene.

Activities

14 Read Scene 6, page 15. Consider the purpose of the 'Freeze and replay' idea in the middle. What does this tell us about Russ? Why does he desire to replay events? How does Russell's final speech change the mood?

15 The mirror is a key symbol in the play, though it is used in different ways with different characters.

- Read the beginning of Scene 12, page 32. What aspect of DJ's character does the mirror emphasise here?

- Read Scene 16, page 45. The scene opens with Craig looking into a mirror saying, 'Whatta you looking at? You're pathetic'. Explore what the double meaning of this may be. On the surface what does it appear Craig is doing? On the other hand, what does it symbolically reveal about the way he may feel about himself? How does this contrast with the image Craig has made for himself?

- Read Scene 19, page 52 in which Russ's reflection comes out of the mirror and speaks to him. This entire scene can be read symbolically. What part of Russ do you think his reflection might represent? What change in Russ do you think this suggests?

- Consider the reasons why Scene 22, page 58, is called 'Mirror, mirror'. What is the obvious reason? Think about what the scene reveals about the main characters.

Self-image in literature

Long before Shakespeare's plays, characters in stories have been concerned with their image and the way they are seen by others. Think about the Greek myth of Narcissus and his obsession with his own reflection.

Activities

16 Read the extract below from *An Inspector Calls* by J. B. Priestley. This play was written in 1945 but set before the First World War when there existed huge social class divisions. In this extract, Mr Birling, a wealthy businessman, and his family are celebrating the engagement of his daughter, Sheila, to Gerald who comes from a very rich and influential family:

Birling lights his cigar and Gerald, who has lit a cigarette, helps himself to port...

BIRLING: [...] By the way, there's something I'd like to mention – in strict confidence – while we're by ourselves. I have an idea that your mother – Lady Croft – while she doesn't object to my girl – feels you might have done better for yourself socially —

Gerald, rather embarrassed, begins to murmur some dissent, but Birling checks him.

No, Gerald, that's all right. [...] But what I wanted to say is – there's a fair chance that I may find my way into the next Honour's List. Just a knighthood, of course.

GERALD: Oh – I say – congratulations!

BIRLING: Thanks. But it's a bit too early for that. So don't say anything. [...] You see, I was Lord Mayor here two years ago when Royalty visited us. And I've always been regarded as a pretty useful party man. So – well – I gather there's a very good chance of a knighthood [...]

17 In a small group, discuss:
- What social class do Birling and Gerald come from. What clues are there?
- What part of his image is Birling most proud of?
- What is Birling concerned that Lady Croft may feel about him and his family?

18 With your group, try acting out this extract. Take turns acting and directing so you can evaluate your performances. Use the following tips to help you:

- Think about how the characters would speak to reflect their high social class.

- How would you use posture, mannerisms and voice to show Birling's confidence, pride and arrogance?

- How can Gerald's awkwardness be conveyed?

19 In a small group, discuss stereotypical images of the elderly. In your group, put together a series of four still-life pictures showing different situations where an elderly person rebels. Try to show how the people around would react to this behaviour.

20 Now, with your group, devise a short poem (10–12 lines) where a character rebels against the image expected of them; e.g. a bully being nice, a weakling standing up for him/herself, a teacher misbehaving, etc.

21 Devise a presentation for your class using the poem as the narration. Decide how best to show the action, e.g. using still-life pictures or mime. Take turns narrating the lines.

Y7: S&L18; Y8: S&L16; Y9: S&L11,12

THEMES AND ISSUES

The body beautiful

Read the following extracts and notes.

'My friend Sophie and I were in the car earlier today reading beauty magazines and J-Lo was plastered everywhere. It was like 'Ooh, no, go away. We want your body but we won't achieve it.' It's just the whole image thing now. It's a really bad message to send out – that's everybody's got to be perfect… No, I can't be bothered, that's why I'm not interested in most of the film projects put to me. The producers say, 'You'll have to lose weight.' So I say, 'OK, I don't want your role then.' I'm a normal size but all actresses, whenever you see them in the flesh are tiny, absolutely tiny, because the screen puts so much weight on you.'

Singer Charlotte Church

The Hollywood film *Shallow Hal* starring Gwyneth Paltrow as a grossly overweight character appears to poke fun at this obsession with weight, and seems to reinforce the message that it is the person inside that counts. However, as part of our research we asked a 15-year-old student, Anna Wardell, to review the film for us. Her conclusions are very interesting:

'The film explores the issue of image and physical attraction according to weight. Hal falls for a woman who is extremely fat but he sees her as slim, implying that size is irrelevant to attractiveness. However, I think that the film still puts across the subliminal message that 'slim is beautiful' because the woman is made to **seem** thin for him to fall in love with … the film appears to say "Size doesn't matter, it's personality that counts, but it would still be better if you were thin!" '

In India, most actresses cast in the so-called Bollywood films, are between size 12 and 14, much larger than their American counterparts. Ironically, Rene Zelleweger, one of Hollywood's top actresses, was paid an estimated $15 million dollars to put *on* a stone in weight in order to resume her role in *Bridget Jones's Diary*. The media's fascination with her subsequent weight loss seemed to only reinforce Hollwood suggestions that skeletal is beautiful.

And it isn't always the female stars who are under pressure to conform to a certain Hollywood image. In the film *Troy*, Brad Pitt plays the Greek warrior Achilles. However, even though Pitt is extremely famous for his good looks, his legs have been deemed too puny for the role. A more muscular body-double has been used in certain scenes, although his upper body has not been doctored.

Activities

1 Discuss in pairs (one boy and one girl): Who do you most admire on television or in films? Why do you like them?

2 Do you sympathise with the views of Charlotte Church? Why do you think film producers say to many aspiring actresses, according to Charlotte, 'you must lose weight'?

3 Why do you think producers decided to 'replace' Brad Pitt's legs in the film *Troy*?

4   Do you think it is easy or difficult for Charlotte Church to be herself without worrying about what others think?

Body image and history

According to teacher Jane Parker in Scene 11, page 31, Socrates constantly stopped people in the streets of ancient Greece and asked them questions such as 'What is beauty?'. It would be interesting to hear what answers he would get today. However, the current obsession with slender waists has not always been fashionable or popular.

In Tudor England, the perfect Elizabethan beauty would be judged by her complexion. A golden tan was NOT desirable, but not because of any health concerns. A tanned face was often associated with the lower classes who spent their time working outside in the fields. Therefore, fashion-conscious Elizabethans preferred to stay in the shade. It was very fashionable to have a deathly pale face and neck, sharply contrasting with bright red lips and red spots on the cheeks. This was often achieved by rubbing the face and neck with deadly poisonous white lead, producing the white effect so desired by many ladies, but often leading to severe damage to the skin. Eyes also had to be large and shining and to achieve this effect, sometimes the juice of deadly nightshade berries was used, again highly poisonous.

In Nazi Germany, posters showed what Adolf Hitler thought a woman's life should be – as a housewife and a mother. Their role was to produce as many children as possible. The 'natural look' was very much favoured and teenage girls were discouraged from following fashion. Make-up and wearing trousers were also discouraged. Girls were not allowed to dye their hair or wear it long and loose. Most chose to have their hair in a bun or plaits. Slimming was also discouraged because the Nazis considered that slim people were not suited to having many children. The ideal male in the Nazi Youth movement was also blond, blue eyed and muscular. Strength was everything, weakness despised. The Nazis also banned films and magazines from Europe and the United States which they considered to be unsuitable. The popular Hollywood films featuring Tarzan the apeman were banned in Germany in 1933 because Tarzan and Jane were dressed in skimpy costumes showing a lot of flesh.

Activities

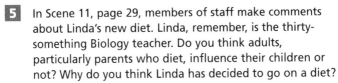

5 In Scene 11, page 29, members of staff make comments about Linda's new diet. Linda, remember, is the thirty-something Biology teacher. Do you think adults, particularly parents who diet, influence their children or not? Why do you think Linda has decided to go on a diet?

6 Find a selection of full length or half length portraits painted by artists between 1500 and 1800. Your art or history teacher may be able to help, also the internet can provide many useful images. You may include both males and females. Now compare these pictures with images found in modern magazines. Note any differences in size, weight, expression, etc.

7 Based on the above information, produce a poster advertising a new Elizabethan beauty salon, showing the range of new products available.

Stereotypes

Blondes

Hollywood actress Reese Witherspoon has enjoyed enormous success playing the character Elle Wood in the *Legally Blonde* films. Her character is initially mocked and derided as an 'airhead' and yet she ends up going to college and gaining a law degree. In the Hollywood dream sequence in *Face Value*, DJ gets the main lead in a fictitious film called *Eternally Blonde*.

Here are the views of two blonde girls of differing ages:

'Absolutely loved *Legally Blonde*. Reese Witherspoon was fantastic, her character should be a role model for girls everywhere. She's sweet, friendly, gorgeous but not totally perfect which means you can't help but like her. I think it's a huge advantage being blonde. Not only do you get to play the bimbo image, so no-one minds when you get confused and it takes double the time to understand a joke, but you also get to shock everyone when they realise you do have more than two brain cells and can string a sentence together.'

FRAN, aged 18, who achieved the highest marks in the AS

History examination at her Sixth Form College in Cambridge last year.

'I have no problems with being blonde. Yes, there are the jokes but I don't take them seriously. I definitely get more attention — especially from the boys.'

KEHL, aged 15.

Lads

During one of the episodes of the BBC television comedy series *Men Behaving Badly*, the two male characters, Gary and Tony, are discussing 'male words' and 'girly words'. Examples given are:

■ Male words: penalty shoot out, carburretor

■ Female words: flip flops, dewberry

Activity

8 Why do you think blonde girls are often portrayed as 'bimbos' or 'brainless'? Do you think there are any advantages in being blonde for a girl? Discuss.

9 Imagine you are a stereotypical 'lad' or 'ladette'. List ten examples of 'male' and 'female' words or expressions.

10 *Men Behaving Badly* is funny because it deliberately stereotypes male behaviour. But how are they behaving badly? Are they robbing banks or beating people up? Of course not. So what types of behaviour do you think the writer had in mind when he created the characters for this series?

11 In *Face Value* we expect Craig to always be 'hard'. Give three examples from the play of how he demonstrates this with his language and behaviour.

12 In the 'Mirror, mirror' scene, page 58, Craig is very unhappy to start with when he finds out he has to join the drama group. Why is this?

13 Craig shows more enthusiasm when he is offered the part of the wolf. Unfortunately for him, he gets little chance on stage to prove his acting ability. Write an additional scene in which Craig gets to play the part of the wolf, reacting with one or two other characters. Instead of 'stereotyping' the wolf's behaviour, be imaginative and look at other ideas. For example, the wolf might be a gentle and helpful creature, he/she may be a vegetarian, or scared of the dark. Let the wolf's words and body language reflect this new development.

Surgery

In the 'Mirror, mirror' scene, page 58, Snow White (DJ) advises her 'ugly' stepmother that she is in need of drastic surgery to improve her looks, including liposuction and breast implants. In Scene 9 of the play, page 21, the class are asked to come up with definitions for the perfect male and female forms.

A recent survey of teenage girls carried out on an internet site revealed that three quarters of girls aged between 12 and 14 say they would like cosmetic surgery as they believe this would help them improve their looks, feel happier about themselves and stop teasing and comments by friends. Only one in four said they were happy with their looks.

Pop star Michael Jackson has repeatedly claimed that he has not undergone massive surgery to alter his looks, but the evidence appears very unconvincing.

Activities

14 In pairs or groups of four, draw and label what you think makes a perfect female and male body

15 In the same groups, discuss: What conclusions can you draw from the resulting pictures? Are there any similarities?

16 Write down four things that worry girls about their body image. Write down four things that worry boys about their body image.

17 Look at the following ways given to improve body image. Discuss the value of each one and give a mark out of ten.

- a new hairstyle
- cosmetic surgery
- regular exercise

- buying new clothes/shoes
- make-up
- going on a diet
- eating more healthy foods, salads/vegetables/pasta
- going to bed earlier
- taking steroids
- hanging around with good-looking boys and girls

Add two more to the list.

18 Would you consider ever having cosmetic surgery? Can it ever be justified? Would you ever consider cosmetic surgery for fame?

Fame

Three years ago, school girl Jenna Mansfield became headline news when she asked for breast implants as a sixteenth birthday present. Jenna had decided that it was the only way for her to become 'famous' and work in television. She quoted a number of examples, including TV presenter Melinda Messenger. Later she decided to put off the operation until she was older.

Activities

19 In *Face Value*, Destiny Jade, wants to be famous but never actually explains what she wants to do. Would you like to be famous? Try and define what being famous or being a celebrity actually means.

20 In groups, discuss the advantages and disadvantages of being famous and then list five people today who are famous, giving the reasons for their fame. Do they have anything in common? What do you think you actually **need** in order to be come famous today?

21 Research. Most television presenters, especially in entertainment programmes, tend to be young. A few presenters, like Michael Parkinson, Desmond Lynham and Robert Kilroy, are grey-haired and over 60. But how many female presenters are aged 60 or over and still appear regularly on our screens in this country? Can you explain why this should be?

22 Now look at the list of people below, who were judged to be famous over the last 200 years.

- Bob Hope
- Elizabeth Garret Anderson
- Marilyn Monroe
- Captain Scott
- Edward Jenner
- Salvadore Dali
- Richard Arkwright
- Maureen Connolly known as 'Little Mo'

Find out why they were famous. Are there any connections between these people and those that appeared on your original list?

 23 Write a fact file for one of the people above.

24 Will Young was the first winner of *Pop Idol*. Over 30,000 people auditioned throughout the country. Ten made it through to the final. At that time they were all household names, but apart from Will Young, how many other finalists can you name from this competition? What lessons can you learn from programmes like *Pop Idol* and *Fame Academy*?

Accessories

Apart from good looks, DJ also loves clothes and accessories. 'Everyday's like Christmas Day for me,' she says looking at the image tree in Scene 3, page 9.

Activities

25 Design your own image tree and hang on it 10 different items or accessories that you consider to be really important for either a boy or a girl today. Discuss why you made your choice and why.

26 Even DJ recognises that these items cost money and she gives advice about putting trainers in the washing machine to give them the appearance of being new. What other advice could you give to teenagers on how to save money but still look good?

 If you could keep just **one** item of clothing or accessory what would it be and why?

Image and the media

The way we perceive ourselves is very often influenced by the mass media that we are exposed to every day, particularly television, film and magazines. We can often unconsciously receive messages about what we are meant to look like, how we should behave and what we should aspire to. This can sometimes be a positive thing, but it may equally have a negative effect.

Eighteen-year-old student, Hana Moazzeni, feels that the media are largely to blame for creating the myth about image, particularly magazines aimed at teenage girls:

'Magazines tend to use models of a certain type: thin, perfect skin, wearing stylish clothes and generally looking beautiful. Teenagers compare what they look like to what magazines are portraying as normality. Seeing beautiful models scattered across the pages of magazines are bound to affect girls.'Oh why can't I look like her?' 'She's beautiful and I'm so much fatter than her!' Girls naturally compare themselves with models and the models always look — immaculate, perfect. Therefore, many teenagers will consider that they are uglier or fatter than the models. They may lose confidence in their looks or strive to change their image through strict dieting to try and mould their bodies into a shape that is said to be 'right' or 'perfect' by society. The media constructs a false world of expectations on what to look like in order to be beautiful. Also, people spend their money on thousands of products related to looks and body image.'

Although born in the United Kingdom, Hana is part Iranian and frequently visits Iran where life is very different for teenage girls. Some girls can watch pop programmes and fashion shows from the West on satellite television, but they are not supposed to. Such programmes are banned in Iran. Also, girls must cover themselves in public and wear the traditional hijab at all times when they leave home. Far from finding this restricting, Hana welcomes the chance to wear the hijab when she visits Iran. She explains why:

'I enjoy wearing it because it gives me a break from Western life where there is an underlying pressure to look good when you leave your house. In Iran, no-one sees what I am wearing beneath the overcoat (hijab) so it doesn't matter what I put on underneath. I find it much more relaxing to be able to get up and not style my hair and, in a sense, liberating to be able to wear clothes in public that if you wore in the streets of England you'd get funny looks and laughter. I doubt the hijab is seen as relaxing or liberating for Iranian girls who live there all the time, but I choose to visit Iran, so in a sense I choose to wear the hijab. For Iranian girls, there is no choice.'

Below are a number of typical headlines which you can see daily on the covers of magazines. Most are aimed at women and young girls, but some are also for men.

BIKINI BODY IN JUST TWO WEEKS!

EAT YOUR WAY TO THE PERFECT BODY

SIX PACK TO BE PROUD OF — SIX **STEADY ON BOYS! NEW WONDERBRA GIRL TAKES THE PLUNGE.** S I M P L E E X E R C I S E S !

Activities

28 Conduct a class survey about what types of magazines your classmates read. Devise a simple key that you can use (e.g. F = fashion mags; FB = football mags, etc).

- Are there any particular types of magazine that are overwhelmingly popular?
- Is there a difference between what boys and girls read?

29 Carry out a second survey to find out what it is that your classmates most want from magazines, e.g. entertainment, advice, information, etc.

30 Now, each person should give a score for how seriously they regard the magazines they read: 1 = Very seriously; 2 = Quite seriously; 3 = Not seriously at all.

Look at your results. How do your scores add up? Is there a greater proportion of one over another? Are there differences between boys and girls?

31 As a class, discuss how necessary certain magazines are to us. Are they merely a way of passing the time or do they have a greater significance? What purpose do 'lifestyle' magazines like *Hello*, *OK*, *J17* or *Mizz* serve?

32 In pairs or groups, look at a collection of magazines aimed at both males and females. Note how many adverts or articles deal with body image and improvement. Next, survey daily newspapers from one week and note how many references there are to body shape and image, especially in connection with celebrities. Collate the results for each category.

33 In a small group, look at the magazine cover below.

Discuss the following:

- What type of magazine is it?
- What is the target audience?
- Look at the image of the model on the cover. What message do you think this is sending to readers?
- Look at the summary of the articles on the cover. According to this magazine, what is essential for every man?

34 As a class, discuss what might be the positive and negative effects of this type of magazine on an ordinary person. For example, how might they feel looking at the model on the cover? What is the use of language on the article summaries meant to do?

35 With a partner examine the advert below, which is typical in many magazines.

- What product is being advertised?
- What is the main method used for selling this product? What does the advert suggest will happen if you buy this product?
- How are the models portrayed?

- Why might someone want to buy this product? How does it propose to 'change your life'?

- Can you think of any other adverts or commercials on TV that use similar methods to sell their product?

36 With your partner, make a list of the image given to men and women in adverts.

- What are the differences?

- Are there similarities?

- How do you feel about these images? Are they realistic? Do they have a positive or negative effect?

37 Now devise an advert for either a perfume or after-shave that doesn't use the stereotypes of the perfect man or woman. It can either be comic or serious. You may even want to parody the standard adverts you see in magazines.

Self-esteem

The negative feelings that some people have about their appearance and image are often far from reality and may end up damaging their self-esteem and hurting them.

What is so special about having self-esteem?

- Having self-esteem means having the confidence to be an individual and to be yourself. This means saying and doing what you think is right instead of merely trying to impress other people to be part of the 'in-crowd'.

- Having self-esteem also means having a balanced and honest view of the positive and negative aspects of yourself. You are not expected to be perfect, but with a balanced view you can value yourself as a person.

Activities

38 Working in a group, construct a spider diagram showing what you understand about the phrase 'having self-esteem'.

- You could begin with the following suggestions: 'pride in your achievements', 'standing up for yourself'.

- Now, using your ideas, draw the outline of two characters from *Face Value*: one with low self-esteem and one with high self-esteem.

- Around your two figures, write down any words or phrases which show the symptoms of high or low self-esteem. For example:

low self-esteem = feeling depressed about appearance

high self-esteem = less self-conscious/awkward

39 Using the character of Craig, examine with a partner how low self-esteem works. Craig presents a certain image of himself to others which is very different from his reality.

- Use the following scenes to remind you of the image Craig creates for himself: Scene 4, Scene 7, Scene 8 (pages 11, 18, 21).

- The following scenes show the reality of Craig: Scene 15, Scene 22 (pages 43 and 58).

- Discuss what Craig does to hide his low self-esteem. Is this an effective disguise? Have you seen this happen in real life?

- Draw a picture of the two sides of Craig. Divide a page into two columns: on the left side draw the half of Craig with the **image** he has created; on the right side draw the **reality** of Craig.

40 Our self-esteem can often mistakenly be based on false ideas. In a small group, discuss the following statements deciding if they are true or false. It may be difficult to come to a decision about some of these statements.

- 'Thin is beautiful, fat is ugly.'

- 'People with "perfect" looks have nothing to worry about.'

- 'There is a perfect size and shape.'

- 'Most of the people around you have the perfect size and shape.'

- 'Our goal in life should be to be funny, popular and good looking.'

41 In your group, look at the facts and statistics below. Discuss what you think they may show about society's attitude to image:

- The UK now has 3.5 million anorexics and bulimics.
- In the UK, one in 250 teenagers will develop an eating disorder.
- Approximately 150,000 women die of anorexia every year in the USA.
- In 1995 a psychological study found that looking at pictures of models in a magazine for 3 minutes caused 70% of the women participants to feel guilt, shame and depression.
- Every year approximately £10 billion is spent on cosmetics and toiletries worldwide.

42 One way of building your self-esteem is to know yourself better and to be more aware of your own strengths and weaknesses. The more self-aware you are, the more confidence you can begin to have in yourself. Attempt the following activity by yourself to see how much of yourself you really know:

- Divide a page into four equal sections
- In each section put one of these titles:

  My friends' view of me.

  My parents' view of me.

  My teachers' view of me.

  How I see myself.

- In note form, fill in these sections as honestly as you can.
- When you have done this, try to evaluate what you have written. What does this tell you about yourself? Do other people see you the way you see yourself? Are you happy with the way you see yourself? Is this a problem? Does it matter if others have a different view of you?

43 Working by yourself, devise a leaflet aimed at raising the self-esteem of teenagers, particularly about their appearance and image. Use some of the ideas below for sections in your leaflet:

- What are the effects of low self-esteem?
- Why do we sometimes feel so bad about ourselves?
- What can you do to feel better about yourself?

- What is important in life and what isn't?
- Useful statistics and facts (see section on page 94).

Remember that the tone you write in should be positive and non-judgmental. Your aim is to make people feel better about themselves.

AUTHORS' VIEWS ON CHARACTERS

Destiny Jade dropped out of her A-level course to pursue a career in modelling. She appeared in several magazines before moving to Hollywood where she aimed to become a film actress. She managed to get one minor role in a B movie but no other parts after that. Disillusioned she moved back to Britain. She is now married to Nik, who does something in the City. They live in a mock-Tudor 5 bedroomed detached house in Saffron Walden and DJ now owns her own health and beauty salon called *Your Destiny*. The couple, who also own a villa in Marbella, have a five year-old daughter called Poppy Honeydew who is the under sevens Karaoke champion in East Anglia. Destiny no longer has any contact with her former school friends. She drives a Range Rover and a silver grey MX5. She hates pantomimes, especially Snow White.

Ruby became more confident after leaving school and began to appreciate her own qualities. She gave up trying to look and act perfect all the time. She studied psychology at Liverpool University and now works as a primary school teacher in Reading. She lives with her partner Mark and drives a hatchback. Ruby is now a qualified wolf handler and most weekends takes visitors on supervised walks with the wolves through the woods of Berkshire. Ruby is currently planning a school reunion next year and hopes to see DJ again, to thank her for giving her the courage and opportunity to stand up for herself. Last Christmas, she produced the school pantomime.

Craig is unable to keep any job for very long. He finds it difficult to take orders or follow instructions; he considers it weak to do what people ask him. As a result he is often argumentative with his employers resulting in him being dismissed. Craig lives by himself in a council flat with his Rottweiler. He hasn't married or had a girlfriend. He sometimes goes to the dog races but is usually alone. He no longer sees the people he knew in school. No one really bothered to keep in touch with him.

Russ is a librarian and now knows lots more long words to confuse people with. He has a wife and tries to teach his three-year-old daughter Kung Fu. In his spare time, Russ is in charge of the village amateur dramatics group where he somehow always gets the lead roles. He is hoping to be spotted by a talent agent and get his own series on TV. He no longer worries about being ordinary... well, at least not all the time.

Acknowledgements

The publishers would like to thank the following for permission to use copyright material. Every effort has been made to trace copyright holders and to obtain their permission for the use of copyright material. The author and publishers will gladly receive information enabling them to rectify any error or omission in subsequent editions.

TextL p79 Reproduced from *An Inspector Calls* by J. B. Priestley (copyright © Estate of J. B. Priestley 1947 is reproduced by kind permission of PFD on behalf of the estate of J. B. Priestley; p80 *Night & Day* magazine, The Daily Mail © Atlantic Syndication

Photos: p90 Man © Picture Arts/Corbis; p91 Perfume bottle © Image State/alamy.com; Couple © Chad Ehlers/alamy.com